GIVE 'EM HELL

HELL

The Tumultuous Years of Harry Truman's Presidency, in His Own Words and Voice

TERRY GOLWAY

sourcebooks
mediaFusion

Published by Sourcebooks MediaFusion, an imprint of Sourcebooks, Inc.
P.O. Box 4410, Naperville, Illinois 60567-4410
(630) 961-3900
Fax: (630) 961-2168
www.sourcebooks.com

Golway, Terry
  Give 'em hell : the tumultuous years of Harry Truman's presidency, in his own words and
voice / Terry Golway.
      p. cm.
  Includes bibliographical references and index.
  1. Truman, Harry S., 1884-1972—Political and social views. 2. Presidents—United
States—Biography. 3. United States—Politics and government—1945-1953. 4. United
States—Politics and government—1945-1953—Sources. I. Title.
  E814.G65 2011
  973.918092—dc22
  [B]
                                    2010050946

             Printed and bound in the United States of America.
              VP 10 9 8 7 6 5 4 3 2 1

To Arthur Carter, who loves to give 'em hell.

Contents

Part Three: A Term of His Own, 1949–1953

On the CD

The audio on the accompanying compact disc has been selected by the author to enrich your enjoyment of this book, to allow you to experience the words of Harry Truman in his own voice. These selections represent some of the most remarkable moments of his presidency and offer a window into the mind of the man. At the start of each chapter in the book, you will find an icon and track number denoting the corresponding speech on the CD. We encourage you to use, and we hope you enjoy, this mixed-media presentation of the life of Harry S. Truman.

1: First Presidential Address to Congress • *April 16, 1945*

2: National Radio Broadcast Announcing Germany's Surrender • *May 8, 1945*

3: Radio Address Announcing the Surrender of Japan • *September 1, 1945*

4: Speech to the Nation • *January 3, 1946*

5: Jackson Day Address • *March 23, 1946*

6: Address to Congress • *May 25, 1946*

7: Radio Address on Lifting Price Controls on Meat • *October 14, 1946*

8: Speech to the United Nations General Assembly • *October 23, 1946*

9: State of the Union Speech • *January 6, 1947*

10: Speech to Joint Session of Congress • *March 12, 1947*

11: Commencement Speech at Princeton University • *June 17, 1947*

12: Radio Address on the Taft-Hartley Act • *June 20, 1947*

13: Speech to the NAACP, Washington • *June 29, 1947*

The future president grew up in small-town middle America,
far from the urban centers of power in the east.

Harry S. Truman, 1884–1972

HARRY TRUMAN WAS BORN ON MAY 8, 1884, IN THE SMALL TOWN OF LAMAR, Missouri, about a hundred miles south of Kansas City. His mother, Martha Ellen Young, and his father, John A. Truman, lived in a small home with no indoor plumbing, across the street from a barn where John traded in mules. John Truman was thirty-three years old in 1884; Martha was thirty-two, having married at the relatively advanced age of twenty-nine. Harry was their first child, although Martha, or Mattie, as everybody called her, had a stillborn child in 1882.

The Trumans and Youngs had a deep attachment to the fields of Missouri and the streets of Kansas City. They were farmers with fresh memories of the brutal Civil War that tested their sense of identity and ideas of freedom in a state bitterly divided between Confederate sympathizers and Union loyalists. Mattie's parents, Solomon and Harriet Young, owned large parcels of land in Missouri's Jackson County. They were slave-owners but they remained loyal to the Union after Southern states seceded in late 1860 and early 1861. Their sympathies did not help them, however, when Union forces marched through the heavily contested border region during the war's early stages. Union soldiers made off with corn, livestock, and supplies from the Young family's farm, to the everlasting fury of Mattie Young, who was nine years old at the time. She would continue to tell stories of Union depravity in decades to come, even after the rest of the world had moved on to other wars and other outrages. Her brother, Will, left home as a young man to serve in the Confederate army.

John Truman's parents, Anderson Truman and Mary Jane Holmes, received two slaves—a mother and daughter—as a wedding present from Mary Jane's mother in 1846. They settled in Kansas City, a fledgling town with ambitions of becoming an important center for trade and commerce as the young United States continued to expand westward. The Trumans, like the Youngs, sided with the Union, but they saw little of the conflict and terror that scarred other counties in Missouri.

The Civil War cast a long shadow over the lives of both families, united through the marriage of John Truman and Mattie Young in 1881. John and Mattie's firstborn son, Harry, grew up hearing tales of a conflict that pitted neighbor against neighbor and cut short so many lives. Harry would grow up with a keen appreciation of history and an abiding interest in the exploits of generals and armies, a reflection, perhaps, of the stories he heard about his country's most devastating war.

Harry Truman's parents, Martha Ellen Young and
John A. Truman, were married in 1881 in Missouri.

Harry Truman was named in honor of an uncle on his mother's side, Harrison Young. When he was just fifteen years old, Harrison Young was nearly lynched by marauding Union soldiers who rampaged the family home in search of the young man's father, Solomon Young. Harrison was the oldest male on the premises—his father was away on business—and when the teenager insisted that his father was nowhere to be found, the troops strung him up but decided not to hang him.

Harry's middle initial was just that, an initial. His parents couldn't decide whether to name him in honor of Solomon, his maternal grandfather, or his paternal grandfather, Anderson Shipp Truman. They decided to give him just the initial, S.

Harry Truman would one day describe his childhood as idyllic, a Mark Twain novel come to life in the fields of Jackson County. His appreciation of history and his sense of the past were shaped by the stories his parents and grandparents passed down about life among their pioneer ancestors during the early years of the nineteenth century. Curious and bright, young Harry became a voracious reader of history, not just of his own country, but of the great nations and empires of the past. His parents encouraged him to read and made sure that their home did not lack for books. Harry's very appearance suggested scholarship, for he began wearing glasses while he was still in grade school. His poor vision and reliance on eyeglasses kept him from the rough and tumble games of his schoolmates, and so he learned to play the piano and developed a love of classical music while the other boys played sports. Although he often told affectionate stories of his childhood and adolescence, he occasionally suggested that life for young Harry Truman was not quite so simple. Childhood, he once said, was a lonely stage of life.

Thanks to his father's ambition, good reputation, and hard work as a livestock trader, the family was prosperous as Harry reached adolescence. They moved to a fine neighborhood in the small town of Independence, Missouri, not far from a frame house owned by the Wallace family on North Delaware Street. Elizabeth Wallace lived there, and Harry met and fell in love with her while they still were in grade school.

———ᘒ———

John Truman introduced his oldest child to politics in the late nineteenth century. The two of them attended outdoor political rallies where orators carried on for hours, bands played, flags flapped in the breeze, and everybody, it seemed, was interested in the issues of the day. Father and son managed to get tickets to the Democratic National Convention in Kansas City in 1900, when the party nominated William Jennings Bryan for president for a second time. Bryan was dubbed "the great commoner," a Midwestern lawyer who spoke to and for the anxieties of struggling farmers who distrusted eastern bankers and city slickers in general. John Truman, however, did not necessarily share the worries of many Bryan supporters. He regularly invested the money he made as a livestock trader, inspiring dreams of a grander house and an affluent future for his family.

Harry graduated high school in 1901 (along with his good friend and future press secretary Charlie Ross, as well as Elizabeth Wallace) and had a dream of his own. Thinking he might make a good soldier and even a great general like Caesar or one of the other heroes he encountered in his never-ending studies of history, he tried for an appointment to the U.S. Military Academy at West Point, not realizing that his eyesight would bar him from admittance. His vision, however, was not an obstacle to other martial pursuits. In 1905 he joined the National Guard, drilling and training on weekends and in the summer, and continued to serve until 1911.

Harry's father's investments in grain futures fell apart not long after Harry left high school, and he was never able to attend college. The Trumans literally lost everything—their land, home, and savings. Harry went to work to help his family, starting as a bank clerk in Kansas City. When his father needed help working on a farm owned by his in-laws, Harry quit the bank and city life to spend his days behind a plow, carrying out the endless chores of a farmhand.

He reconnected with Elizabeth Wallace, known to her friends as Bess or Bessie, in 1910. They socialized, talked about books, and gossiped about mutual friends. Bess's mother Madge did not approve, believing that Harry Truman was not good enough for her daughter. Harry summoned the courage to propose marriage—in a letter. Bess turned him down, and Harry feigned relief. "I never was fool enough to think that a girl like you could ever care for a fellow like me but I couldn't help telling you how I felt," he wrote. "I have always wanted you to have some fine, rich-looking man, but I know that if ever I got the chance I'd tell you how I felt even if I didn't ever get to say another word to you."[1] Bess must have been charmed, although it took a while. In 1913, two years after Harry proposed, Bess agreed that they should be married. No date was set, but the two considered themselves engaged.

Harry continued to work the farm with his father until John Truman died in 1914, after undergoing surgery for an intestinal blockage caused by a hernia. Harry, always thinking of the good life he hoped to make for Bess, sought to better his fortunes by investing money his mother loaned him in a zinc mine. He lost it all when the venture fell apart, but the farm provided a good income, and Harry did not suffer as his father did when his investments soured.

———— ❧ ————

War, far more catastrophic than the one the Trumans and Youngs so bitterly remembered, broke out in Europe in 1914. The main impact on Missouri was positive—prices for grain and other foodstuffs rose as the Allied powers of Europe looked to America to feed their armies. The United States remained neutral, although clearly in sympathy with Britain and France, until 1917, when a German submarine offensive against American shipping prompted President Wilson to ask Congress for a declaration of war against the Central powers. Harry Truman, at age thirty-three, signed up for another tour with the National Guard. His fellow guardsmen elected him as a first lieutenant in recognition of his enthusiasm and his organizing skills, even though he had yet to fire a shot in anger and his only knowledge of military matters came from books, not from experience. Truman's unit was absorbed into the American Expeditionary Force under the overall command of fellow Missouri native General John J. Pershing. He sailed for the battlefields of France in April 1918, was promoted to captain, and was given command of Battery D, 2nd Battalion, 129th Field Artillery. Captain Harry Truman was an unlikely field officer and he knew it, but he quickly won the respect of his troops, who learned that he would not hesitate to discipline slackers. Harry was a soldier's soldier and never asked his men to do anything he wouldn't do himself.

Battery D went into action on the western front in late August and was part of the vast American offensive at Saint-Mihiel in mid-September. The Allied powers, on the verge of catastrophic defeat months earlier, took advantage of the influx of hundreds of thousands of American troops like Harry Truman. By early November, the Central powers were in retreat. The guns fell silent on November 11, 1918, with the Allies victorious. Captain Harry Truman and his men had been part of a brutal, bloody campaign and had helped turn the course of the war. He and the men of Battery D would be friends for the remainder of their days.

Truman insisted before he left for France that he and Bess wait until the war was over before they married, just in case, he said, he returned home incapacitated—if he returned at all. He didn't wish to be a burden on Bess or leave her a young widow. He thankfully returned safely from the war, and Harry Truman and Elizabeth Wallace were married on June 28, 1919, in Independence. After a brief honeymoon, the happy couple returned to Independence, moving in with Bess's mother on North Delaware Street. Harry Truman would never buy his own home—for him, home would always be Madge Wallace's house.

Elizabeth Wallace, better known as Bess, was Harry Truman's childhood sweetheart. They married on June 28, 1919.

After the wedding, the groom and a friend, Eddie Jacobson, went into business together, opening a men's clothing store in Independence in 1919. Truman & Jacobson offered quality merchandise, and both men worked hard to make the business work. But by 1922, the partners were deeply in debt. Jacobson declared bankruptcy, but Truman did not. He would repay his obligations over the next two decades.

Harry moved from the clothing business to politics in 1922 at the suggestion of an Army buddy named Jimmy Pendergast, scion of the Irish-Catholic family that ruled Kansas City's famed political machine. The Pendergasts needed a candidate for county judge, a job that entailed oversight of county spending and contracts, not, as the title suggested, courtroom responsibilities. Truman agreed, won election easily (as all Democrats did in Jackson County), and began his political career on January 1, 1923, not long after Truman & Jacobson dissolved. Although Truman never planned a political career, he enjoyed the work of county judge, settling into his new career and earning praise for his efficiency and integrity. He and Bess became parents in February 1924 when Bess gave birth to a baby girl. They called her Margaret.

By the early 1930s, Harry Truman, now the chief judge of Jackson County, was being mentioned as a possible candidate for governor of Missouri. He was not displeased, for he had grown to enjoy politics and government, and learned that he was good at both. Well into middle age— he was on the verge of turning fifty—Harry Truman had found his calling.

And now his calling found him. In 1934, to his astonishment, the powerful Pendergast machine decided that Judge Harry Truman would make a good candidate for United States senator—after, that is, several other candidates turned down a chance to run on the Democratic line. Truman had reason to be surprised, for the Pendergasts had refused to support Truman's plan to run for the House of Representatives in 1934. But with a senate line open and other leading Democrats uninterested in the nomination, Truman's old friend Jim Pendergast suggested to his powerful uncle, Tom Pendergast, that Judge Truman might make a fine senator. The elder Pendergast was skeptical, but he agreed. Truman won a hotly contested primary for the party's nomination but won easily in November. He was on his way to Washington.

Truman won a place in national politics in 1934 as he
campaigned for a U.S. Senate seat from Missouri.

Franklin Roosevelt was in the middle of his historic first term as
president when Truman arrived in the Senate. FDR could not have found a
more reliable ally than Truman, who instinctively supported the president's
expansion of federal government programs, including the Social Security
Act and the Wagner Act, which protected labor unions. He defied the
White House, however, in supporting antilynching legislation that FDR
quietly opposed in order to keep his white Southern supporters in line.

Other senators treated Truman as if he was an intruder, for he was perceived as representing not the people of Missouri but the family-run machine
that ruled Kansas City, the Pendergasts. Truman's undoubted connection to
the machine—he would always consider Jim Pendergast a friend—became
an even greater liability in 1939, when Tom Pendergast was indicted on
federal tax charges. The disgraced boss pled guilty and was sent to prison.
The popular governor of Missouri, Lloyd Stark, announced that he would
challenge Truman's reelection bid in a Democratic primary in 1940. So did
the local federal prosecutor, Maurice Milligan, who helped put Pendergast
behind bars. Harry Truman was considered an almost certain loser when the
campaign, one of the most remarkable in U.S. history, got underway.

But he didn't lose. Campaigning as if his career depended on the outcome—and it did—Truman outworked his two opponents in the cities and farms of Missouri. He won by fewer than ten thousand votes. Had he faced a single opponent, he might well have lost and returned home to Independence, a failed one-term senator.

His new term had barely begun when Harry Truman proposed the creation of a special Senate committee to investigate mounting evidence of corruption, graft, and incompetence in the federal government's mushrooming military contracting process. Europe was already at war, and Franklin Roosevelt was doing all he could to arm Britain for an expected German invasion, while at the same time beefing up the U.S. military in case the worst happened. The White House and top Senate leaders agreed on the need for such an investigation, so in March, a new committee, the Senate Special Committee to Investigate the National Defense Program, was created. Everybody called it the Truman Committee, as Senator Truman was the man in charge.

The Truman Committee conducted hundreds of hearings, issued dozens of reports, and earned its chairman a reputation as a fair-minded and well-prepared legislator, rather than the image of a hack politician fronting for a corrupt political machine. The committee found evidence of shoddy work by defense contractors and bureaucratic bungling in federal agencies. The investigation continued even after the nation entered World War II on December 7, 1941, and the civilian economy was transformed to accommodate the demands of total war. Truman and his committee members continued to question defense contractors and bureaucrats alike, looking for waste and corruption, relentless in their pursuit of greater efficiency in the name of the men and women in the armed services. Harry Truman, derided during his first term as the "Senator from Pendergast," found his colleagues more respectful now. His personality certainly helped change minds too. He was a good social mixer, intelligent without being pompous, a political animal who could be friendly with members of the opposing party. But it was his work on the committee that unofficially bore his name that separated him from his colleagues. As biographer David McCullough noted, political correspondents named Truman one of the top ten people in Washington who helped win the war. He was, McCullough wrote, the only member of Congress in that group.

With daughter Margaret and wife Bess, Harry Truman hit the campaign
trail in 1944 as Franklin D. Roosevelt's running mate.

As Franklin Roosevelt prepared to seek a fourth term in 1944, advisors
and political observers turned to the question of a running mate. Incumbent
vice president Henry Wallace was unpopular with the party's bosses, who
thought he was too liberal and unreliable. Behind the scenes, one of FDR's
key political advisors, Edward J. Flynn of the Bronx, began plotting to
remove Wallace from the ticket. Flynn and other urban bosses decided to
push Harry Truman as a replacement. FDR wavered as the party prepared
to decamp to Chicago for its national convention, but finally agreed to dump
Wallace in favor of Truman. The senator from Missouri was astonished—he
was preparing to nominate Senator James Byrnes of South Carolina, widely
regarded as the favorite to succeed Wallace. But FDR's advisors, led by
Flynn, worked the delegates to ensure Truman's nomination on a second
ballot. In November, Harry S. Truman of Missouri won election to the
nation's second-highest elected office and was sworn in as vice president on
January 20, 1945.

During the next four months, the new vice president spent a good deal of time in the Senate, attending to his constitutional duties as president of the body that he loved. He rarely discussed anything of importance with his boss, Franklin Roosevelt, but when they did meet, he surely would have noticed the president's shocking appearance. He was terribly thin, with deep, dark circles under his eyes. He was dying. And on April 12, 1945, Franklin Roosevelt collapsed and died while on a working holiday in Warm Springs, Georgia. Harry Truman was now president of the United States.

He was a startling contrast to his beloved predecessor, the only man to serve more than two terms as president. Roosevelt endeared himself to millions of Americans with his fireside chats, delivered in a distinctive Hudson Valley accent that reflected his privileged upbringing. Truman, on the other hand, spoke in a flat Midwestern accent, his speech—and his speeches—unadorned and straightforward. Americans had barely gotten to know Truman and hearing him on the radio, speaking from the Oval Office, was disconcerting after twelve years of Franklin Roosevelt.

Truman inherited a crushing burden of unfinished business. Americans were at war in Europe and Asia, and while an end was in sight, the U.S. and its allies had only begun to plan for a postwar world. Scientists were at work on a breathtaking weapon of mass destruction, a development Truman knew nothing about until he became president. Domestic planners were worried that peace and the return of millions of American men to the home front might spark another terrible depression or ruinous inflation. And a new conflict with an old ally, the Soviet Union, loomed as tensions increased between Moscow and Washington.

And now all of this was in the hands of Harry Truman, a high school graduate from a small town in Missouri, a stranger to the world's great leaders. Over the next four years, Harry Truman made a series of vital decisions, explained in frequent speeches to the American public, which shaped the postwar world. He ran for reelection in 1948 and was written off as a sure loser. American voters supposedly clamored for change, but in one of the most stunning upsets in U.S. history, he defeated his Republican rival, Thomas Dewey, to win another term. During the next four years, Harry Truman remained in the forefront of global politics, the first man to bear the title of leader of the free world in a globe divided between West and East. He committed the United States to a new war in Korea, and pressed a reluctant Congress to expand on Roosevelt's popular New Deal reforms.

The Korean War brought down his popularity though, and in 1953, he left office to a general sigh of relief. This time the nation really did want change, electing Republican Dwight Eisenhower as president rather than Truman's choice as his heir, Adlai Stevenson. Truman remained an active elder statesman through the 1950s and into the 1960s as Democrats sought him out for photo opportunities and policy advice. He died in his home town in 1972 at the age of eighty-eight. But in death, Harry Truman gained new life in American political circles. His candor, his plain way of speaking, came into vogue after years of scandal and official lies in Washington. He was the subject of several well-received biographies and was even lionized in a pop music song by the group Chicago.

Bess Truman lived to see her husband returned to the pantheon of great American presidents. She died in 1982. Their daughter, Margaret Truman Daniels, wrote a bestselling biography of her father before turning to a series of mysteries. She died in 2007, triggering the nation to stop yet again to recall the astonishing career of a plain-speaking man from Missouri who led the nation during the apogee of the American century.

PART ONE:
An Accidental President, 1945–1946

Truman prepares to take the oath of office
after Franklin Roosevelt's death.

Introduction

FEW PRESIDENTS HAVE CONFRONTED SO MANY PROBLEMS AND MADE SO MANY decisions in their first year of office as Harry Truman in 1945. Less than a month after succeeding Franklin Roosevelt, Harry Truman announced to a relieved nation that Nazi Germany was beaten, ending the catastrophic war in Europe. He turned his full attention on winning another war, this one in Asia, while simultaneously preparing the nation for demobilization and a return to a civilian economy. Truman's most momentous decision came in the summer, when he authorized the use of atomic bombs over the Japanese cities of Hiroshima and Nagasaki. Japan announced its surrender after the second attack, and the war came to an end.

Victory brought new anxieties, about inflation, about a return to high unemployment and low growth, about renewed tension between labor and management. While peace and victory were satisfying, they brought no respite for the Truman White House. The domestic front was anything but jubilant and content. Unionized workers in key industries, free from agreements to avoid strikes during wartime, walked off the job in record numbers, challenging Harry Truman's commitment to workers. The president found management just as intransigent.

Abroad, the wartime alliance with the Soviet Union fell apart amid intense acrimony. Truman looked on in approval when Winston Churchill, the former British prime minister, criticized the Soviet Union for constructing an "iron curtain" to divide East from West. A Communist insurgency in China threatened to topple a key U.S. ally and give Moscow an important strategic victory in the opening rounds of a new war—the Cold War.

When American voters went to the polls in 1946 for congressional elections, they seemed anything but a triumphant, hopeful people. Strikes, a housing shortage, and increasing tension abroad led them to throw out the Democratic leadership on Capitol Hill. The midterm election was an enormous defeat for Harry Truman, one that seemed to foreshadow an even bigger defeat in 1948.

Truman and a grief-stricken Anna Roosevelt, the late president's
daughter, prepare to board the funeral train
at Union Station in Washington.

CHAPTER 1

A Heavy Heart

First Presidential Address to Congress
April 16, 1945

TRACK 1

O N THE RAINY AFTERNOON OF APRIL 12, 1945, THE U.S. SENATE WAS DEEP IN discussion of a proposed treaty with Mexico concerning water rights in the Rio Grande and Colorado River. Vice President Harry Truman followed the debate from his new perch as the Senate's presiding officer, making parliamentary rulings and otherwise keeping the debate orderly and civil. Not all vice presidents embraced this mostly ceremonial role, but Truman enjoyed the opportunity to be with his former Senate colleagues from both parties. He was a popular figure on Capitol Hill, where he earned a reputation for candor, integrity, and hard work.

As the treaty debate droned on, Truman busied himself not with Senate work, but with a letter to his mother and sister back home in Missouri. He discussed the weather in Washington (beautiful until the rain arrived that day), the ongoing discussion taking place on the floor (one of the senators, he said, was "windy"), and his upcoming radio address to the nation, scheduled for the following night. "I think I'll be on all the networks, so it ought not to be hard to get me," he wrote.[1] Truman was pleased to remind his mother and sister that when he finished his formal remarks, he would introduce the next speaker, President Roosevelt, who was scheduled to deliver a short address from his retreat in Warm Springs, Georgia.

Truman had not seen a great deal of the president since Inauguration Day, January 20. Roosevelt was in Yalta on the Crimean Sea in early February, meeting with Winston Churchill, the British prime minister, and Soviet leader Joseph Stalin. Since his return, Roosevelt and his vice president had met twice for private sessions, but the president chose to reveal little. Truman could not fail to note the president's appearance: he was thin and pale, with great dark circles under his eyes, looking like a man who needed a very long rest. He left Washington for Warm Springs in late March, hoping that the better weather and more relaxed atmosphere would revive him in time for the opening of the first United Nations conference in San Francisco in April.

When the day's tedious Senate debate came to a welcome end that Thursday afternoon, Truman retreated to the private office of Texas congressman Sam Rayburn, the powerful Speaker of the House of Representatives. Rayburn hosted a daily after-work cocktail party for selected friends and colleagues in an office he and his guests called the "Board of Education." Truman, who enjoyed bourbon and water, was a fixture at these gatherings, even after earning his promotion to the vice-presidency.

Truman walked to Rayburn's office from his own office in the Capitol and the Speaker was there to greet him. While Rayburn, a genial host, mixed Truman's drink, he told him that Steve Early, President Roosevelt's press secretary, had called and asked that the vice president call the White House.

Truman returned the call immediately. Early had an urgent request. "Please come over," he told Truman, "and come in through the main Pennsylvania Avenue entrance."[2] Early did not say anything more, but Truman gathered from his tone of voice that this was not a routine request. He excused himself, sought out his driver, and rode the short distance from Capitol Hill to the White House.

Eleanor Roosevelt and other members of the Roosevelt family were waiting for him. The first lady greeted him not with a handshake but by putting her hand on his shoulder. "Harry," she said, "the president is dead."

Earlier that afternoon, Franklin Roosevelt suffered a cerebral hemorrhage while attending to routine paperwork and sitting for a portrait in Warm Springs. He lingered for two hours. While Harry Truman was jotting off his note to his mother and sister, Franklin Roosevelt was sprawled on a bed in his retreat, unconscious. He died at 3:45 p.m., just as the Senate was wrapping up its proceedings for the day.

Shocked, Truman still managed to ask the president's widow if there was anything he could do for her. Mrs. Roosevelt, who lived in the White House longer than any other first lady and who was intimately familiar with the burdens of the presidency, was even more gracious. "Is there anything we can do for you?" she replied. "For you are the one in trouble now."[3]

Harry S. Truman was sixty years old on that rainy day in April 1945. A plain-speaking son of the American heartland, he could hardly have been more different from the patrician New Yorker whose place he would now take. Although he was astonishingly well-read, he never attended college. Franklin Roosevelt was a graduate of Groton and Harvard and the scion of Hudson Valley aristocrats. Roosevelt was charismatic and charming; Truman was friendly and blunt. Roosevelt understood the power of the spoken word and knew how to use his voice to convey intimacy with audiences numbering in the millions. Truman spoke in a flat staccato, his sentences devoid of the imagery that made Roosevelt's speeches so memorable.

The nation barely knew Harry Truman. In the weeks since becoming vice president, Truman was not in the news very much, but when he was, it was for all the wrong reasons. Within days of his inauguration, Truman flew home to Missouri to attend the funeral of his friend Tom Pendergast, the famed—or infamous—political boss of Kansas City. Pendergast died in disgrace after having served five years in prison on corruption charges. Truman's presence at the funeral raised questions about his judgment and served as a reminder that, unlike his disinterested, reform-minded boss Roosevelt, Harry Truman was a creature of urban-machine politics. The Pendergast funeral seemed to confirm the judgment of critics who rolled their eyes when Truman emerged as FDR's running mate at the Democratic National Convention in 1944. National magazines questioned his competence, experience, and his friendship with political bosses. Now that man was president of the United States and commander in chief of an army of millions.

A two-front world war was nearing an end, and when peace finally arrived, the United States found itself in a position of power as the world's great victor and liberator. Wisdom, maturity, and, more than anything else, experience were required to see the war to a successful conclusion. The public associated those qualities with its president of more than a dozen years. They were not among the virtues attached to the name of Harry S. Truman in 1945.

So, as Mrs. Roosevelt said, it was Harry Truman who was in trouble now, as the burdens of a burgeoning superpower were placed upon his shoulders. He would later tell reporters, "I felt like the moon, the stars, and all the planets had fallen on me."[4]

Truman was aware that he was destined to look small, parochial, inexperienced, and simply not good enough. "There have been few men in all history the equal of the man into whose shoes I am stepping," he said the following day, April 13. "I pray [that] I can measure up to the task."[5]

Truman took the oath of office in the White House just after seven o'clock, with his wife, Bess, daughter, Margaret, and several cabinet members and White House staff looking on, each of them grief-stricken.

The new president asked FDR's cabinet to remain, at least for the time being, and decided to move forward with plans for the UN conference in San Francisco. Later that night, he received a briefing from the secretary of war, Henry Stimson, who told his new boss that the nation was developing an extraordinary new weapon. Stimson did not offer any more details, and Truman did not ask for any.

As the country mourned, Harry Truman, seemingly one of the most unlikely presidents in American history, moved into the Oval Office filled with Franklin Roosevelt's memorabilia and personal touches. He cleared a spot on the presidential desk but otherwise tried to disturb nothing. Like many of his fellow citizens, Harry Truman had a hard time thinking of anybody except Franklin Roosevelt leading the country. When a reporter said, "Good luck, Mr. President," Truman replied, "I wish you didn't have to call me that."[6]

As the country prepared to pay final tribute to its fallen leader, the new president sat through briefings about the war's progress and the problems that would follow Germany's defeat. The future of Poland, destined to become a major flash point in the postwar settlement, was already causing tensions between the Soviets and the Anglo-American allies. Truman met frequently with the secretary of state, Edward Stettinius, a man he barely knew, to get up to speed on international relations, not Truman's strong point during his Senate career.

While the new president sat through these tutorials in global politics, he also had a public role to perform as the nation's chief public mourner at Franklin Roosevelt's funeral. The dead president's body was brought by train from Georgia to Washington, D.C., on Saturday morning, April 14. Truman met the train as it pulled into Union Station and followed a horse-drawn caisson bearing Roosevelt's casket from the station to the White House. Truman saw men, women, and children lining the broad avenues of the capital, weeping as the flag-draped casket passed by. Some could hardly remember a day when Franklin Roosevelt was not president of the United States.

Funeral services took place in the East Room of the White House. In place of a eulogy, the presiding cleric, Bishop Angus Dun, read the most famous line in FDR's first inaugural address: "Let me assert my firm belief that the only thing we have to fear is fear itself." The following day, Sunday, April 15, Truman and his wife, Bess, were aboard a train that took Roosevelt's body from Washington to Hyde Park, where the man who led the nation out of the Depression and nearly through a world war was laid to rest in a simple ceremony.

Truman had not yet addressed the nation. The extent of his public commentary was a written proclamation announcing Roosevelt's death to the world. Now, however, with the funeral rituals complete and Roosevelt buried, it was time for the new president to introduce himself to the nation. He sat with one of FDR's legendary speechwriters, Samuel Rosenman, and with South Carolina senator James Byrnes during the train ride back from Hyde Park, and together they drafted a speech Truman planned to give the following day to a joint session of Congress. The new president realized that an era had come to an end that morning when the body of Franklin Roosevelt was placed in a grave and commended to eternity. A new era was about to begin. It was important that Harry Truman speak to a grief-stricken nation and an anxious world.

The speech, to be broadcast on radio to the nation, was scheduled for one o'clock. It was a beautiful spring day in Washington. Truman, an early riser, hoped to make a few last-minute changes in the speech, but pressing business, especially the ongoing dispute over Poland, commanded his attention. A buzzer rang in the Oval Office at around noon, a signal that it was time to leave for Capitol Hill. There would be no more revisions to his speech.

Harry Truman, so recently a cherished colleague and member of the United States Senate, entered the House chamber just after one o'clock. Senators, representatives, and other government officials rose and offered him a rousing standing ovation. As the applause began to fade, Truman looked down at his speech and began to speak. A voice quickly cut him off. Speaker Sam Rayburn, seated behind the chamber's main podium, said in a stage whisper heard in millions of living rooms, "Just a minute, Harry, let me introduce you."[7] It was, as Truman biographer David McCullough observed, a moving, genuine moment amid the carefully choreographed rituals of power. It also offered Americans a peek at Truman's casual, every-day persona—surely nobody could picture Rayburn addressing Truman's predecessor as "Franklin."

Once he was properly introduced, Truman paid tribute to his legendary predecessor. "It is with a heavy heart that I stand before you, my friends and colleagues," he said. "Only yesterday, we laid to rest the mortal remains of our beloved president, Franklin Delano Roosevelt. At a time like this, words are inadequate. The most eloquent tribute would be a reverent silence." And so official Washington paused one last time to reflect on a memorable and historic life.

Truman then made it clear that life had to go on, and that the policies and legacy of the fallen leader would be continued. "Tragic fate has thrust upon us grave responsibilities," he said. "We must carry on. Our departed leader never looked backward. He looked forward and moved forward. That is what he would want us to do. That is what America will do."

There would be, he said, no change in American war aims. The goal continued to be the unconditional surrender of Germany and Japan. The goal for the postwar world was also the same—not a return to isolationism, but active American engagement and international cooperation. "In this shrinking world," Truman said, "it is futile to seek safety behind geographical barriers. Real security will be found only in law and in justice." Truman's sentiments were aimed at those in his audience who believed, somehow, that the United States could retreat from world leadership after the war, relying as in the past on the oceans to provide a defense against enemies from abroad.

Throughout the speech, Truman invoked the memory of Franklin Roosevelt, insisting that Americans would assist the victims of war and would face new problems with the same sort of "faith and courage which Franklin Delano Roosevelt always had." The nation's efforts to build a just and lasting peace, he said, would be a tribute to the nation's war dead and to the memory "of our fallen president."

It was his commitment to a United Nations organization, however, that best affirmed his role as steward of Roosevelt's vision. While isolationists were hard to find after the Japanese attack on Pearl Harbor on December 7, 1941, Truman understood that many Americans still were skeptical of the Old World and of international institutions. So he made a special plea for support. "I appeal to every American, regardless of party, race, creed, or color, to support our efforts to build a strong and lasting United Nations organization," he said. "To destroy greedy tyrants with dreams of world domination, we cannot continue in successive generations to sacrifice our finest youth. In the name of human decency and civilization, a more rational method of deciding national differences must and will be found."

Truman closed with words he wrote himself, words that only a modest man from the nation's heartland could have written. He drew upon a lifetime of reading to recall a biblical phrase attributed to King Solomon.

"At this moment," he said, "I have in my heart a prayer. As I have assumed my heavy duties, I humbly pray Almighty God, in the words of King Solomon: 'Give therefore thy servant an understanding heart to judge thy people, that I may discern between good and bad; for who is able to judge this thy so great a people?' I ask only to be a good and faithful servant of my Lord and my people."

President Truman left the House to thunderous applause. The man from Independence had the country behind him as he sought to finish the work of his beloved predecessor.

At long last, Harry Truman tells the nation
that the war in Europe is over.

CHAPTER 2

The Flags of Freedom Fly

National Radio Broadcast Announcing Germany's Surrender
May 8, 1945

TRACK 2

ARRY TRUMAN WORKED LONG INTO THE NIGHT DURING HIS FIRST WEEKS AS president, learning on the job as he presided over the climactic stage of the war in Europe. Franklin Roosevelt could not have kept him less informed than he was, to the astonishment of, among others, Winston Churchill. "It seemed to me extraordinary...that Roosevelt had not made his deputy and potential successor thoroughly acquainted with... the decisions which were being made," Churchill wrote in his memoirs of the war.[1] The prime minister added cryptically that Truman's on-the-job training "proved of grave disadvantage...How could Mr. Truman know and weigh the issues at stake at this climax of the war?"[2]

He could learn, and he did. Aides noted that the president was a quick study as they brought him up to speed on the war's progress, and on preparations for a new world order in which the dominant powers would be the United States and the Soviet Union. Victory over Nazi Germany was certain with each passing day in April 1945. Far less certain was the map of postwar Europe.

Relations between the Anglo-American allies and the Soviets were growing tense even before Roosevelt's death. The Red Army had liberated Poland from the Nazi regime, and the Soviets installed a Communist-dominated government there. Under the Yalta agreement, that government was to be reorganized and made more inclusive, with representatives from the Polish government who were in exile in London as well as other non-Communist officials. The agreement called for free and fair elections as soon as possible, but not long after Roosevelt returned from Yalta, it was clear that the Soviets had little intention of allowing anything but a one-party Communist government to take root in Poland. A furious Roosevelt told Churchill that neither he nor the American people would "support participation in a fraud...[The] solution must be as we envisaged it at Yalta."[3]

Harry Truman had not been privy to that vision. And as that vision became imperiled, Truman found himself at the center of a foreign-policy crisis that threatened to split the alliance, even as it neared victory over Nazi Germany. Truman barely knew his secretary of state, Edward Stettinius; he had never met his ambassador to the Soviet Union, Averell Harriman; and he was certainly a stranger to the world of grand global strategy.

Still, decisions with far-reaching consequences had to be made, and Harry Truman had to make them. Within forty-eight hours of becoming president, he and Churchill sent a joint message to Stalin emphasizing that the pro-Soviet government in Poland had no right, as it insisted, to decide which Polish civilian leaders would be invited to Moscow for consultations concerning a new government. In the meantime, Churchill urged Truman's support for a plan that would have allowed British field marshal Bernard Montgomery to push deep into Germany and take the capital, Berlin, before the Soviets could. The Allied supreme commander, Dwight Eisenhower, opposed the plan, arguing that Berlin had no military significance. Truman supported Eisenhower, and so, to Churchill's chagrin, Montgomery's 21st Army Group remained well west of Berlin as the Soviets prepared for the final, crushing blow.

It was, to say the least, an extraordinary time to be thrust on the world stage as commander in chief of the world's mightiest nation. Harry Truman was in a position he never sought. The vice-presidency, his stepping stone to the White House, was thrust upon him at the 1944 convention, not because he was considered a natural successor to Roosevelt, not because he was steeped in the great issues of war and peace, but because the party's shrewd urban bosses regarded him as dependable—a "solid man," in the vernacular of the Democratic machines. But though Truman had not sought out the presidency, he stepped up to take the job and was actively proving his worth. Even leftist muckraker I. F. Stone confessed that Roosevelt had been right to dump Henry Wallace from the ticket in favor of Truman. "At this particular moment in history," Stone wrote in *The Nation*, "Mr. Truman can do a better job."[4]

Truman's family was also affected by his unexpected rise to the presidency. In April 1945 he wrote a letter to his mother and sister and apologized to them for any inconvenience they might be suffering because of his exalted position. "It is [a] terrible—and I mean terrible—nuisance to be kin to the President of the United States," he wrote. "I am sorry for it, but it can't be helped."[5] The president then turned his attention to the war, and to the continuing battle with Stalin over Poland.

Truman became increasingly impatient with his ally in Moscow even as Allied troops put the finishing touches on the defeat of the Nazi regime. On Monday, April 23, the Soviet foreign secretary, Vyacheslav Molotov, was scheduled to arrive at the White House for a meeting with Truman and his foreign policy team while on his way to the United Nations conference in San Francisco. The new president had been briefed by, among others, U.S. Ambassador Harriman, who flew to Washington from Moscow to warn Truman about Soviet intentions in Eastern Europe. Harriman described Stalin's power grab in Poland and elsewhere as a "barbarian invasion"—a highly undiplomatic turn of phrase, and one that caught Truman's attention.[6] It seemed clear, the president wrote years later, that "the Russians intended to try to force this puppet government [in Poland] upon the United States and England."[7] Truman was concerned that if the Soviets did not abide by the Yalta agreement in Poland, American public opinion could turn against U.S. participation in the new United Nations organization. That, Truman believed, would be a catastrophe.

Truman's military and foreign policy advisors were divided over how tough a line the president ought to take with Molotov. Some of his military aides were concerned that any confrontation might persuade the Soviets to sit out the war in Asia, since the American military were counting on their aid as an invasion of Japan loomed. The diplomats, like Harriman, were less willing to placate Stalin. They believed the Soviets were intent on establishing puppet regimes not only in Poland but throughout Eastern Europe.

Molotov arrived at five thirty and was quickly escorted to the president's office. Truman already had a reputation for running efficient, no-nonsense meetings and this one was no exception. Once Molotov was seated, Truman dispensed with pleasantries—the two men had actually met briefly the night before when the president formally welcomed the foreign minister to the country—and got right to business. The United States, Truman said, would not support formation of a government in Poland that did not include non-Communist leaders, including members of the Polish government in exile. He handed Molotov a letter outlining Washington's insistence that Moscow consult with representatives of all democratic factions in Poland before forming a new provisional government. The United States, Truman said, had agreed to a plan for Poland's future. It was up to the Soviet Union to abide by that agreement.

Molotov was visibly shaken, according to several reports. In Truman's account, Molotov took offense to the president's tone. "I have never been talked to like that in my life," Molotov said, according to Truman's account in his memoirs.[8]

"Carry out your agreements and you won't get talked to like that," Truman quoted himself as replying. Though this exchange has never been corroborated, there is general agreement that the meeting between Truman and Molotov was anything but polite, and that Truman made his annoyance quite clear. Molotov left the White House without having to parse the president's words for hidden meanings.

As relations among the anti-Nazi powers deteriorated, their armies moved closer to victory and, as they squeezed Berlin from east and west, they bore witness to their enemy's crimes against humanity. The first large concentration camp to fall into the liberator's hands was Bergen-Belsen, near the town of Celle in northwest Germany. In late April, Winston Churchill received a message through diplomatic channels that Heinrich Himmler, head of the dreaded Nazi SS, met with a Red Cross official and offered to surrender all forces under his command on the western front. He insisted though that the war against the Soviets would continue, and indeed, he expected the Allies to join the Germans in that battle. Churchill called Truman—top-secret transatlantic telephone lines were a marvel of the age—to report the offer. They turned it down, of course, and Churchill forwarded the information to Stalin. Regardless of the tensions between the

Anglo-American allies and the Soviets, any attempt to play the Allies against each other was doomed to failure.

Himmler's offer was one of the final, desperate acts of a dying regime. Adolf Hitler knew the war was lost and that the unimaginable atrocities carried out in his name against Europe's Jews would soon be exposed. On April 25, U.S. and Soviet troops linked up near the village of Leckwitz on the River Elbe in central Germany. Newsreel photographers recorded the historic moment: American GIs and Red Army veterans shaking hands and exchanging pleasantries, united in common effort against one of humanity's most wretched regimes.

Germany's collapse continued in late April. Russian troops were on the verge of encircling Berlin, tightening the noose as Hitler and his aides awaited the inevitable in a bunker underneath Berlin. Hitler demanded to know when he could expect a counterattack against the Russians, who already were in the capital. There were no reinforcements to answer his call. Adolf Hitler shot himself the following day, April 30.

―――∽―――

The war was not over, but many Americans at home assumed it was. Truman told the nation during a press conference on May 2 that German units continued to fight on despite Hitler's death and the battle was still underway. While that was true, the rumors of peace were not entirely wrong. They were simply premature.

On May 7, 1945, German General Alfred Jodl surrendered what remained of his country's armed forces. As word of the surrender reached Britain and the United States, civilians and soldiers alike prepared to celebrate. Behind the scenes, however, the Anglo-American allies and Soviets were once again locked in a bitter dispute. Churchill proposed that all three allies announce the war's end at six o'clock that evening, May 7. Stalin, however, objected, because Germans on the eastern front had yet to lay down their arms. He believed the official victory announcement should wait until May 9. To add to the confusion at this climactic hour, German foreign minister Count Schwerin von Krosigk announced on radio that his country had surrendered. Newspapers printed extra editions with gigantic headlines announcing the end of the war in Europe. War-weary civilians and battle-hardened veterans alike waited for an official announcement from the victorious capitals. But Truman's press secretary, Jonathan Daniels, told reporters that he had nothing to announce.

To Churchill's chagrin, Truman decided to accommodate Stalin's request to hold off official announcement of the war's end. The prime minister, who was bursting to address his countrymen, learned of Truman's decision during a phone call with Admiral William Leahy, the president's chief of staff. "In view of agreements already made," Leahy told Churchill, "my chief asks me to tell you that he cannot act without approval of Uncle Joe"—Anglo-American shorthand for Stalin.[9] A frustrated Churchill cancelled plans to speak to his fellow Britons that evening, May 7. Instead, he and Truman would declare victory the following day, May 8—coincidentally, Truman's sixty-first birthday. Stalin remained adamant about May 9, and as a result, the Russians celebrated their victory a day after their allies did.

On the last official night of the war in Europe, May 7, Harry, Bess, and Margaret Truman formally moved into the White House after spending the weeks since Roosevelt's death in Blair House, across the street from the executive mansion. Truman allowed Eleanor Roosevelt as much time as she needed to move from her home of more than a decade. Army trucks carted Mrs. Roosevelt's possessions from Washington to Hyde Park; a single truck moved the Trumans from Blair House to the White House on May 7.

The following morning was V-E Day, a day for celebrations and thanksgiving as the war in Europe came to an end. Truman rose early, as usual, dashing off another letter to his mother and sister. "I am sixty-one this morning," he wrote, "and I slept in the President's room in the White House last night."[10] The president met with reporters at 8:30 a.m. in the Oval Office. They were uncharacteristically quiet and solemn as Truman read a statement acknowledging what so many people knew already—that the German surrender was complete, and the war in Europe was over. "The flags of freedom fly all over Europe," he said.

———— ಌ ————

At nine o'clock, the president addressed a worldwide radio audience from the diplomatic reception room in the White House. His speech was similar to the statement he read to the press half an hour earlier, but in this version, he added a tribute to his predecessor.

"This is a solemn but a glorious hour," he began. "I only wish that Franklin D. Roosevelt had lived to witness this day. General Eisenhower informs me that the forces of Germany have surrendered to the United Nations." Truman's use of the phrase "United Nations" referred not to the international organization that was, even at that moment, being born in San Francisco. During the war years, the Allied nations used the phrase "United Nations" to refer to the alliance against Nazi Germany.

Truman's tone was somber rather than celebratory, for, as he noted, victory had come at tremendous cost. "Our rejoicing is sobered and subdued by a supreme consciousness of the terrible price we have paid to rid the world of Hitler and his evil band. Let us not forget, my fellow Americans, the sorrow and the heartache which today abide in the homes of so many of our neighbors—neighbors whose most priceless possession has been rendered as a sacrifice to redeem our liberty."

V-E Day, he reminded listeners, would not put an end to sacrifice. Victory over the Nazis meant liberation for millions and an end to suffering in Europe, but the freedom of millions more would require more sacrifice, more work, and more tears. "Our victory is but half-won," he said. "The West is free, but the East is still in bondage to the treacherous tyranny of the Japanese." Complete victory, he reminded his listeners, required the unconditional surrender of Japan.

Some of Truman's listeners needed no such reminders. They were huddled around radios in Guam and other U.S. outposts, or aboard battleships in the Pacific. Some were engaged in the bloody campaign to take Okinawa; others were training for the planned invasion of Japan itself, a campaign expected to cost hundreds of thousands of American lives. Their war was far from over.

Truman's speech looked forward to a day when peace would return, not just to Europe, but to the entire world. "We must work to bind up the wounds of a suffering world—to build an abiding peace, a peace rooted in justice and in law," he said. "We can build such a peace only by hard, toilsome, painstaking work—by understanding and working with our allies in peace as we have in war.

"The job ahead is no less important, no less urgent, no less difficult than the task which now happily is done."

With that, the president read aloud from an official proclamation designating the following Sunday, May 13, to be a national day of prayer in recognition of the victory in Europe and the effort that still lay ahead.

The president's address took six minutes to deliver. When he finished, Americans raced into the streets for a celebration that was years in the making, one that would be remembered for decades to come.

On May 9, as the Russians celebrated, Harry Truman returned to the task of not just winning the war in Asia, but winning the peace in Europe.

The Japanese formally surrender to General Douglas MacArthur
aboard the battleship U.S.S. Missouri.

CHAPTER 3

Peace at Last

Radio Address Announcing
the Surrender of Japan
September 1, 1945

TRACK 3

IN HIS SPEECH ANNOUNCING THE END OF THE WAR IN EUROPE, WINSTON CHURCHILL, the British prime minister, echoed Harry Truman's warnings that victory was not yet full, peace not yet restored. "We must never forget," Churchill said, "that beyond all lurks Japan, harassed and failing, but still a people of a hundred million, for whose warriors death has few terrors."[1] The prime minister's cautionary note was more eloquent than Truman's, but the message was the same. Americans with loved ones serving in the Pacific surely needed no reminder that the celebration of V-E Day marked only the beginning of the end, not the end itself. Harry Truman was less than four weeks into his presidency when the Germans surrendered. The weeks following V-E Day might well have seemed like years for a politician new to the national, never mind global, stage. Presiding over the relentless, brutal war in the Pacific was a daunting challenge, even if, as Churchill suggested, the Japanese effort was failing. But Truman did not have the luxury of devoting all, or even most, of his energy to the Pacific. The problems referred to his attention were, it seemed, beyond counting. With peace came myriad issues, none of them negligible. Europe was liberated but broken. Men responsible for the slaughter of Europe's Jews and other war crimes were in Allied custody, awaiting adjudication. The prospect of peace meant the imminent demobilization of nearly fifteen million men and women—would they find jobs and housing when they returned? Any one of these issues was daunting. Taken in combination, the burdens on Truman were enormous. But there was yet another problem weighing down Truman, one that became increasingly difficult to shoulder as the spring of victory wore on. Relations with the Soviet Union over Poland and Eastern Europe continued to deteriorate as Washington turned its attention to finishing off Japan.

The victory celebrations in Times Square and other public spaces were barely over when Truman received an anxious telegram from Churchill asserting that "in these next two months the gravest matters in the world will be decided."[2] The prime minister reiterated his concerns that the Soviets were intent on imposing puppet governments throughout eastern and central Europe. Churchill feared the consequences of a quick American demobilization in Europe—without a strong U.S. presence, he told Truman, there would be nothing to stop the Soviets from turning half of Europe into vassal states. They agreed that they ought to meet with Stalin again as soon as possible to express their concerns personally. In the meantime, Truman sent FDR's old confidant, Harry Hopkins, to Moscow to see if he could ease tensions before any meeting among the three leaders.

All the while, the murderous, brutal war went on in the Pacific, a war unlike that fought on the western front in Europe. American troops had been horrified to see Japanese civilians killing themselves and their families rather than submit to defeat and occupation in the battle for Saipan in mid-1944. Now, as U.S. troops advanced ever closer to the Japanese homeland, soldiers and civilians alike became even more desperate, even more determined to avoid the humiliation of capture. Japanese civilians by the thousands leaped from cliffs during the bloody battle of Okinawa, which had been raging since the U.S. invasion on April 1. U.S. warships off Okinawa were attacked by a new weapon—the kamikaze pilot, men who deliberately flew their bomb-laden planes into U.S. warships, killing themselves and as many Americans as possible.

For Truman and his military advisors, the Okinawa campaign offered a terrible glimpse of the horrors that surely would accompany an invasion of Japan. More than twelve thousand Americans and more than a hundred thousand Japanese were killed in ten weeks of fighting. Meanwhile, in Tokyo, thousands of civilians were incinerated during the spring of 1945 when U.S. warplanes firebombed the capital night after night. During a single raid in late May, American bombers turned sixteen square miles of Tokyo into ash and debris. The Japanese government was unmoved. The fight would continue, the government promised, until the last Japanese was dead. In the context of the Okinawa campaign, Truman could hardly treat the government's statement as mere propaganda.

Around mid-April, Harry Truman learned that his country was on the verge of developing a weapon unlike any other in human history. Secretary of War Henry Stimson informed the president that, within four months, "we shall in all probability have completed the most terrible weapon ever known in human history, one bomb...which could destroy a whole city."[3] Franklin Roosevelt had kept Truman in the dark about the Manhattan Project—the development of an atomic bomb. Truman now learned that when the time came, he would have to decide whether or not to use this weapon of mass destruction.

In early June, Truman was briefed on the deliberations of a small committee charged with investigating the use of the terrible new weapon under development in Los Alamos, New Mexico. The committee, chaired by Secretary of War Henry Stimson, concluded that the atomic bomb, as yet untested, should be used without warning against a well-chosen target. The committee recommended that war plants ought to be singled out for the attack, but made it clear that mere destruction was not the weapon's sole goal. The devastation, according to the report, ought to "make a profound psychological impression on as many inhabitants as possible."[4] In other words, the bomb should terrorize as well as destroy. If the Japanese government refused to acknowledge reality, perhaps grieving Japanese civilians could force the issue.

The commission's recommendations were not binding. The fate of the new weapon was up to Truman—yet another burden on the new president. "The final decision of where and when to use the atomic bomb was up to me," he wrote in his memoirs. "Let there be no mistake about it. I regarded the bomb as a military weapon and never had any doubt that it should be used."[5] Neither did General George Marshall, the Army's chief of staff and Truman's future secretary of state. Marshall noted that conventional air raids over Tokyo had killed as many as a hundred thousand people, and yet the Japanese government refused to admit defeat. More troops had died on the first day of the invasion of Iwo Jima, a small island near the Japanese home islands, than were killed during the D-Day invasion of France in 1944. Resistance would only become more fanatical in the face of an American invasion of the Japanese homeland, Marshall believed.

Truman was presented with the military's plan for that invasion in late June. Estimates of casualties varied, depending on where the invasion took place. The low estimate for the first month of combat was about thirty thousand American dead. Secretary Stimson believed that a million Americans would die or be wounded before the island nation was subdued. However, the invasion might not be necessary if the Japanese were forced, or persuaded, to surrender in the face of overwhelming destruction. Truman had to choose between terrible scenarios, one of which held out the promise of victory without invasion.

Truman gathered his thoughts and some spare clothes, including a tuxedo, and packed them away as he prepared for his first trip abroad as president. On July 7, 1945, he set sail across the Atlantic Ocean to meet with Winston Churchill and Joseph Stalin in the historic German city of Potsdam, near the smoking ruin of Berlin. Before he left, he accepted the resignation of Treasury Secretary Henry Morgenthau, who had been in the cabinet since 1934. Morgenthau wanted to accompany the president to Potsdam, in part to argue in favor of turning postwar Germany into a central European breadbasket rather than a revived industrial giant. The secretary, however, was not included on Truman's list of invitees. He confronted Truman and threatened to resign, adding perhaps a bit too imperiously that he was more qualified and talented than some of Truman's other cabinet choices. Truman replied by accepting Morgenthau's resignation, effective immediately.

The Potsdam conference was Harry Truman's debut on the world stage. It also served as a poignant reminder that the man who had worked so hard and for so long to achieve victory over fascism and militarism, Franklin Roosevelt, was gone. Americans had become familiar with scenes of Roosevelt seated with the other world giants, Churchill and Stalin, in Teheran and Yalta, talking over great issues of war and peace. Now, it was Truman, not Roosevelt, alongside Churchill and Stalin. The effect must have been jarring, as were some of the developments to come.

The Anglo-American allied leaders met first, for the first time, before deliberations with Stalin began. "I did not feel that I was meeting a stranger," Truman later wrote, although he was disappointed that the great Briton was not "very fond of music—at least my kind of music."[6] The piano-playing Truman was a devotee of classical composers, especially Mozart.

Stalin had yet to appear at Potsdam. He was on his way by train from Moscow, a journey of about a thousand miles, but was behind schedule. The conference was delayed for a day. Truman used the unexpected time off to tour the remnants of Berlin. Along the way, on a deserted highway, he passed the 2nd U.S. armored division. Troops stood at attention and saluted as he passed. The president was soon in Berlin, a smoldering, ruined city from which Hitler had planned a thousand-year reich. Now he was dead, his regime defeated, his crimes uncovered. "I never saw such destruction," Truman wrote.[7]

Later that evening, Truman learned that the potential for delivering even more catastrophic destruction was at his command. The atomic bomb was no longer a theoretical possibility—at about 1:30 p.m. Berlin time, American scientists and military personnel witnessed the dawn of a new era when the world's first nuclear explosion lit up the sky in New Mexico. News of the atomic bomb's successful test was delivered in a coded telegram from Washington. "Operated on this morning," the telegram read. "Diagnosis not yet complete but results seem satisfactory and already exceed expectations." Truman kept this information to himself.

Stalin arrived a day late and made a point of visiting the new American leader before the formal sessions got underway on July 17. Truman was struck by Stalin's size, as the Soviet leader was several inches shorter than Truman. During their conversation, Stalin mentioned almost in passing that the Soviets would enter the war with Japan in mid-August. Truman expressed his pleasure and soon afterwards invited the Soviet to join him and his party for an unscheduled lunch of liver, bacon, and ham. Stalin tried to offer his excuses, but Truman parried them by insisting that if Stalin wanted to stay and eat lunch, he could stay. Stalin, after all, answered to Stalin. The Soviet could hardly resist Truman's challenge, and the two leaders continued their discussion over their modest meal.

Later that afternoon, the conference began in earnest in a palace that had served as a military hospital during the war. At Stalin's suggestion, Truman was named chairman of the conference because, as president of the United

States, he was head of state as well as head of government. (In Britain, the king was head of state; in the Soviet Union, the chairman of the Supreme Soviet, Mikhail Kalinin, was head of state. In the world of diplomacy, heads of state take precedence over heads of government.)

As was his custom at home, Truman ran a brisk, efficient meeting, which seemed to please Stalin, although Churchill preferred more discursive sessions, and it showed. The prime minister did a great deal of talking, leading a frustrated Truman to demand action, not words. "I don't want to discuss," he said pointedly. "I want to decide."[8]

One historic decision, separate from the deliberations at Potsdam, was now his to make. On the morning of July 21, Stimson, General George Marshal, and presidential aide James Byrnes met with Truman behind closed doors to discuss the results of the atomic bomb test. Stimson read a long report that described, in specific detail, the effects of the huge explosion. For Harry Truman, there was little question about what came next. Within a few days, the U.S. military came up with a list of four potential targets for a nuclear attack: Hiroshima, Kokura, Niigata, and Nagasaki. Truman authorized the attack on July 25.

Churchill had been privy to the secret, for the Manhattan Project—the covert effort to build the bomb—included British personnel. Truman, however, assumed that Stalin was unaware, and so he broke the news to the Soviet leader on July 24. Stalin seemed neither surprised nor interested, with good reason. He had known about the project for years, thanks to a spy at Los Alamos.

The Potsdam conference continued, with the good cheer of early sessions giving way to tense discussions over Eastern Europe. Stalin gave no ground, insisting that the British and Americans ought to recognize the new pro-Soviet governments in the region. When Churchill complained that British diplomats in Romania and Bulgaria, both within the Soviet sphere, were under virtual house arrest, Stalin shouted, "All fairy tales!"[9]

On July 25, Winston Churchill flew back to Britain to be on hand when the results of a general election held weeks earlier were announced. Collecting and counting the votes of Britain's soldiers overseas led to the long lag time between Election Day and the final result. Churchill was worried about the announcement, but the rest of his party seemed confident.

Churchill's anxiety was well-placed. To the astonishment of the world,

Britain's voters turned out their war-hero prime minister, choosing the Labor Party and its leader, Clement Atlee, instead of Churchill's Conservatives. The dramatic, shocking change meant that Atlee took Churchill's place for the remainder of the conference. Stalin was now negotiating with two relative strangers.

In the end, the Anglo-American allies failed to win concessions from Stalin over the future of Eastern Europe. While all sides agreed on some issues, including reparations and border concerns, Potsdam was not the triumphant conclusion of an extraordinary alliance, but the beginning, in many ways, of a new war—the Cold War. Truman, new to the world of diplomacy, had hoped that personal contact with Stalin might lead to a change of Soviet policy. The president later admitted that his idea was naïve.

Before the conference broke up under the guise of amiability, Truman, Atlee, and the Chinese leader Chiang Kai-shek issued a statement calling on the Japanese government to surrender or face complete destruction. American warplanes distributed thousands of copies of the statement during flyovers. The Japanese promptly and publicly rejected the ultimatum. On July 31, Truman gave final approval for a nuclear assault to be carried out no sooner than August 2. He wished to be on his way home from Potsdam when the bomb fell.

Hiroshima was incinerated on August 5, 1945, at 7:15 p.m. Washington time. Nagasaki was attacked on August 9. Two cities were destroyed, and hundreds of thousands were either dead or horribly wounded. After Hiroshima, but before Nagasaki, the Soviets declared war on Japan, as Stalin had promised Truman at Potsdam. The Japanese government issued a statement on August 10 indicating that it was prepared to end the war, though there was no mention of surrender. With the neutral Swiss government serving as an intermediary, the Truman administration and the Japanese negotiated over several difficult issues, including the future role of the Japanese emperor, revered as a deity as well as head of state. Finally, on August 14 came word that the Japanese agreed to surrender. The war, at last, was over. Truman, his wife, and his cabinet met with reporters in the White House at seven o'clock that evening to announce the surrender and to commemorate the war's end. Enthusiastic crowds gathered outside the White House and in public places throughout the nation, but Truman insisted that the official celebration of V-J Day (Victory in Japan) would not take place until the Japanese signed an instrument of surrender.

They did so on September 1, 1945, aboard the battleship U.S.S. Missouri. The venue was hardly an accident. Truman decided that the ceremony ought to take place aboard a U.S. ship docked in Tokyo Bay. "I thought it wise to hold the ceremony within view of the Japanese capital in order to impress the fact of defeat on the Japanese people," Truman wrote, "but it also seemed desirable to remain offshore until we could be assured that there would no last-minute outbursts of fanaticism."[10] The U.S.S. Missouri not only was named for the president's native state, but was christened by the president's daughter, Margaret. General Douglas MacArthur, Allied supreme commander in the Pacific, presided over the solemn ceremony, which was broadcast live around the world. Truman, like tens of millions of his fellow Americans, listened to MacArthur's stentorian voice as he announced that "these proceedings are closed." Truman, an avid student of world history, let his thoughts wander to other historic milestones—the defeat of the Spanish Armada in 1688, Wellington's victory over Napoleon at Waterloo, and, of course, the recent fall of Hitler and Nazism. Had the world learned anything from the slaughter and carnage, or was humankind doomed to repeat the mistakes and horror that took the lives of millions? In the midst of these thoughts, Truman heard MacArthur finish his remarks in Tokyo. It was ten o'clock, Washington time. Time for Harry S. Truman to speak to the world.

Truman addressed himself to his "fellow Americans" and to "General MacArthur in Tokyo Bay."

"The thoughts and hopes of all America—indeed of all the civilized world—are centered tonight on the battleship Missouri," he began. "There on that small piece of American soil anchored in Tokyo Harbor the Japanese have just officially laid down their arms."

At this moment of absolute victory, he reminded Americans of how the war started, and the vow they made to themselves. "Four years ago, the thoughts and fears of the whole civilized world centered on another piece of American soil—Pearl Harbor. The mighty threat to civilization which began there is now laid at rest.

"We shall not forget Pearl Harbor. The Japanese militarists will not forget the U.S.S. Missouri."

Truman, in this moment of victory, avoided ringing, triumphant rhetoric. Instead, he tried to articulate the thoughts of war-weary Americans listening in living rooms and parlors across the nation. So many of them, he knew, were thinking of the men and women who would not return from far-flung battlefields. "No victory," he said, "can make good their loss...No victory can bring back the faces they longed to see." Victory in a vast, two-front war cost the lives of more than four hundred thousand Americans. Hundreds of thousands more were wounded. Many of them would never be made whole again. Victory came at a terrible price.

The war was fought on the fields of northern France, on the beaches of the South Pacific, in the jungles of Asia, and high over some of the world's great cities. But, Truman noted, victory required the services not only of troops, but of civilians who sacrificed in the name of nation and of liberty.

The nation's thoughts, he said, went out to workers, businessmen, and civil servants, to the volunteers who worked on draft boards and in hospitals, and to the president who had led the nation for so long, through depression and war. Franklin Roosevelt, he said, was a "defender of democracy" and "architect of world peace and cooperation." The victory they won was unique in the annals of war. Victory brought not conquest, but liberation; not territory, but the spread of universal ideals.

"This is a victory of more than arms alone," Truman said. "This is a victory of liberty over tyranny," won by "the will and spirit and determination of a free people—who know what freedom is, and who know that it is worth whatever price they had to pay to preserve it.

"It was the spirit of liberty which gave us our armed strength and which made our men invincible in battle," he said. "We now know that the spirit of liberty, the freedom of the individual, and the personal dignity of man, are the strongest and toughest and most enduring forces in all the world."

Truman proclaimed the following day, September 2, as V-J Day. After another round of celebrations in America's cities and towns, Harry Truman and the American people would begin the hard work of keeping the peace.

Harry Truman took a special interest in the White House and its grounds. Here, he admires the mansion's garden, which offered him relief from the domestic crises of peacetime.

CHAPTER 4

Managing the Peace

Speech to the Nation
January 3, 1946

TRACK 4

THE UNITY AND GOOD FEELINGS THAT PEACE AND VICTORY PRODUCED WERE short-lived. Around the country, labor unions were beginning to demand higher pay and better working conditions, demands that most workers had put on hold during the war. What's more, some members of Truman's Democratic Party joined with conservative Republicans to thwart some of the new president's policy proposals, including increases in unemployment compensation. Congress and Truman worked well together on foreign policy as war gave way to a disappointing and brittle peace. But on domestic issues, the tensions and disagreements that plagued Franklin Roosevelt's second term returned when Truman made it clear that he intended to build on and expand his predecessor's agenda.

The fall of 1945 ought to have been triumphant in the United States, and, in some ways, it was. The nation was proud of its victory, grateful for the imminent return of millions of men and women, and aware that it had been spared the catastrophic destruction that scarred the cities of friend and foe alike. But victory abroad did not add anything to workers' paychecks. In fact, demobilization led to thousands of layoffs as war orders were cancelled and production of tanks, airplanes, and other material ground to a halt. On September 2 (V-J Day), the government formally cancelled $23 billion in defense contracts. Over the next two weeks, nearly two million civilians were laid off because of the cutback in war spending.

As those pink slips were distributed, the president went to Congress with an extensive and ambitious program of domestic reform that was nicknamed the "Fair Deal." The president called on the services of one of FDR's most prolific speechwriters, Samuel Rosenman, to craft a long address that called for expanding unemployment compensation and benefits for veterans, clearing slums in the nation's cities, building new public works projects modeled on the New Deal's Tennessee Valley Authority, and creating a permanent federal agency to tackle and monitor racial discrimination in the workplace. Truman's Fair Deal program made it clear that he intended to be more than a caretaker of Franklin Roosevelt's legacy. He had an agenda of his own. But powerful forces in both parties did not share Truman's ambitions. Congress politely applauded his speech and then did nothing to advance the Fair Deal. "I'll sure be glad when this terrible Congress goes home," Truman wrote.[1]

The nation's labor unions, given extraordinary power during the New Deal, responded aggressively to layoffs and stagnating wages. Workers in the steel, mining, and automobile industries were especially militant, leading Truman to warn that he would take action to prevent work stoppages in key areas of the economy. He put his warning into action in October when he authorized a federal seizure of more than two dozen petroleum refining plants. But even that drastic action failed to impress restive workers. Just before the nation celebrated its first peacetime Thanksgiving since 1941, nearly 180,000 members of the United Automobile Workers union walked off their jobs at General Motors, the nation's first large-scale strike in years. Smaller labor disputes broke out throughout the country as workers agitated for an end to federal controls on wages. Management also had a grievance with government: it wanted Washington to abolish wartime controls on prices.

The nation had seen similar unrest in 1919, when the close of World War I signaled an end to enforced cooperation and an increase in the demands and needs of both labor and management. Truman wished to avoid a repeat of the divisions and violence that peace brought to the home front when he returned home from Europe's battlefields, but he was baffled by labor's intransigence. He considered himself a friend of the unions, but he was quick to condemn what he viewed as their overly militant attitude toward management and the government. The war might be over, he argued, but troops remained overseas and required supplies. "Nothing will be permitted to stand in the way of the adequate supplies of any kind for our armed forces," he wrote.[2]

In November, the president invited thirty-six leaders from labor and business to a special conference in Washington, D.C., designed to restore cooperation and harmony to the nation's workplaces. Truman personally opened the session with a speech that advocated a genuine commitment to collective bargaining and impartial arbitration to resolve particularly difficult disputes between labor and management. The conferees continued to meet during the next three weeks, leading Truman to cancel plans to visit his mother and sister in Kansas City. Everybody was grating on the president's nerves, including some of his own staff. Congress, he told his mother, was "balking, labor has gone crazy, and management isn't far from insane in selfishness. My cabinet, that is some of them, have Potomac fever. There are more Prima Donnas per square foot in public life here in Washington than in all the other opera companies ever to exist."[3]

Truman's hopes for some sort of truce vanished when union and management delegates to his conference left Washington in early December without an agreement. By then, about half a million American workers were on strike, threatening the oil, mining, and automobile industries. There was talk of a steel strike in early 1946. In early December, Truman delivered a speech to Congress calling for the formation of an impartial fact-finding board. This board would arbitrate labor-management disputes over a mandatory thirty-day cooling-off period, during which labor would agree to remain on the job. Truman asked for quick action from Congress on his proposal.

Congress, however, was not in a mood to act quickly. The mine workers, an important part of Franklin Roosevelt's governing coalition, were utterly opposed to the fact-finding boards, viewing them as a threat to their freedom to strike. Other members of Congress were more inclined to act on legislation that would limit, rather than mediate, labor's power to strike. Truman was equally frustrated with management at General Motors. Although the autoworkers union went along with Truman's appointment of a fact-finding board to investigate the ongoing strike at GM, the company's executives refused to participate. Truman was powerless to compel them. And so the strike continued into the new year, with another potentially crippling strike, this one on the steel industry, threatening to follow.

Truman decided to make an appeal directly to the American people on the night of January 3, 1946, with a national radio broadcast reminiscent of his predecessor's fireside chats. This address, however, lacked the homey, intimate tones of Roosevelt's most famous chats. As the American people were learning, Truman was a very different political animal—he was direct, he was blunt, and he spoke in a clipped staccato that surely seemed jarring to a nation grown accustomed to Franklin Roosevelt's warm, patrician tones.

Truman's unadorned prose certainly had the benefit of clarity. There was no mistaking how he felt. At that time, he felt annoyed and frustrated with Congress and Truman wanted to make sure that both his listeners and the legislators got his message.

He started with flattery. Congress, he said, deserved the nation's congratulations for "carrying out its responsibility in foreign affairs." Congress approved America's membership in the new United Nations organization, fulfilling Roosevelt's dream of full U.S. participation in a global effort to build a lasting peace. Other postwar agreements and treaties were put into place quickly on Capitol Hill, among them the Bretton Woods agreement, which sought to stabilize international markets and currencies. Republicans and Democrats alike showed that the wartime spirit of cooperation had not disappeared with Japan's surrender.

On the home front, however, Truman had only bad news to report. "I wish I could say to you that everything is in perfect order," he said. "I cannot...When we turn to our domestic problems, we do not find a similar record of achievement and progress in the Congress." Capitol Hill's inaction was all the more distressing for Truman because, he said, 1946 had to be "our year of decision. This year we lay the foundation of our economic structure which will have to serve for generations." In the president's view, Congress and the White House had an opportunity to put into place reforms and programs that would further ensure prosperity at home and throughout the world. But doing so required congressional action, and Congress, he said, did not seem inclined to seize the opportunity to "bring about an expanded production and steady, well-paid jobs and purchasing power for all who wanted to work…Reaching that goal means better homes, better food, better health, better education, and security for every citizen of the United States. It means bigger and steadier markets for business. It means world confidence in our leadership."

Truman's attempt to retain a strong hand over the nation's conversion from wartime to a peacetime economy surprised those in Congress who saw the president as a pragmatic moderate who was happy to go along with the program but was not one for visionary initiatives. This radio address, along with Truman's Fair Deal speech several months earlier, made it clear that the president would not be content with simply maintaining the New Deal now that its founder was gone. Instead, he was determined to assert his influence not only in the nation's capital, but on shop floors and corporate boardrooms across the country. So he expanded his attack beyond Congress to include workers and executives who, in his view, put aside public cooperation in pursuit of private gain.

"Immediately after the surrender of Japan, in the full flush of our victory, representatives of the Congress, of industry, of labor, and of farm organization called upon me," he said. "From them I received promises of cooperation and teamwork during this reconversion process. I regret to say that those promises have not all been kept. As a result, many obstacles have been thrown in our path as we have tried to avert the dangers of inflation and deflation."

High on his list of villains was the world's largest carmaker, General Motors, which refused to cooperate with a fact-finding board aimed at ending the dispute between GM and the autoworkers union. He urged Congress to give the board subpoena powers so it could force GM executives to cooperate.

More broadly, Truman told listeners that the wartime system of controls on prices and on rent "will have to be maintained for many months to come, if we hope to maintain a steady and stable economy." His assertion of federal power over the private economy did not end with his request for continued price and rent controls. He asked Congress to act on his previous request for expanded unemployment compensation, an increase in the minimum wage, salary increases for federal employees, and legislation that would "outlaw by permanent statute un-American discrimination in employment." In addition, the country faced an enormous housing shortage that could be resolved with the assistance of government. "Where private enterprise is unable to provide the necessary housing," he said, "it becomes the responsibility of the government to do so." Truman's appointment of a special housing advisor and his promise to build housing where necessary represented another extraordinary expansion of government's role in the private economy, one made possible by the New Deal and by the government's mobilization during the war.

Many of Truman's proposals, save for the housing initiative, were several months old, but were held up because of Congress inaction. The logjam would continue, he said, speaking directly to his audience, "unless you people of the United States" demanded action.

To the president's chagrin, the action that followed his speech was not the sort he intended. Union members were unimpressed with the president's proposals and continued to walk off their jobs, so much so that by the end of January, almost two million Americans were on strike. That figure included the nation's steelworkers, whose threatened strike became reality in late January.

Peace was proving as hard to manage as war.

President Truman and Interior Secretary Harold Ickes had
a strained relationship, which led to Ickes's resignation after
a dozen years in the cabinet.

CHAPTER 5

Life of the Party

Jackson Day Address
March 23, 1946

TRACK 5

ALTHOUGH HARRY TRUMAN WAS A POPULAR FIGURE AMONG BOTH PARTIES ON Capitol Hill during his years in the U.S. Senate, he was still very much a partisan Democrat. That attitude did not change while he was in the White House. Truman was a proud Democrat and a firm believer in Franklin Roosevelt's vision of an activist government working on behalf of the public good.

But Harry Truman was a very different sort of Democrat than Franklin Roosevelt. FDR was a child of the Progressive movement and an acolyte of Woodrow Wilson, the moralistic, idealistic college president turned politician who believed he could make the world safe for democracy. Franklin Roosevelt was elected to the New York state senate at the beginning of Wilson's administration, and he quickly earned a reputation for his opposition to New York City's Tammany Hall, the urban machine controlled by Roosevelt's fellow Democrats. Roosevelt, in fact, was not averse to supporting Republicans who aligned themselves against machine Democrats. He voted for his distant cousin, Theodore Roosevelt, a Republican, in the 1904 presidential campaign, and he quietly supported Republican Fiorello LaGuardia in his successful anti-Tammany mayoral campaign in 1933. Roosevelt even reached out to onetime rivals, especially failed Republican presidential candidate Wendell Willkie, whom FDR defeated in 1940. Roosevelt sent Willkie on a mission to see Winston Churchill after the election, and later considered asking Willkie to be his vice-presidential candidate in 1944 (Willkie died suddenly in early 1944, foiling FDR's vision of a bipartisan ticket).

Roosevelt, who lived off a private family income and who presided over a sprawling estate in New York's Hudson Valley, looked down at bosses like Tammany's Charles Francis Murphy and Kansas City's Tom Pendergast during his early years as an elected official in New York. But as a presidential candidate in 1932 and as president, Roosevelt showed that he had learned something about his fellow Democrats in the nation's cities. Their machines certainly were not pure, but they delivered services and votes, and could be a powerful ally.

If Roosevelt's genius was his ability to weld together moralistic Progressive reformers and practical urban bosses, Truman's task was to keep this important alliance together. The Roosevelt New Deal coalition brought together an extraordinary collection of diverse and competing interests. Included were Southern segregationists and African Americans, farmers and factory workers, Protestant progressives and Catholic bosses, mine workers and Jewish intellectuals. Roosevelt's magnetism as well as the nation's two emergencies—the Depression and World War II—kept this disparate group together for more than a decade. But now Roosevelt was gone, the Depression was long over, and the war would soon be a memory. It was up to Harry Truman to keep the party together as it approached its first postwar test, the midterm congressional elections of 1946.

It would not be easy. Truman's own advisors, or, more properly, the advisors he inherited from Franklin Roosevelt, were becoming restless. In January 1946, Interior Secretary Harold Ickes, a Republican turned Democrat who was an original member of FDR's cabinet, criticized Truman's appointment of an oil man and Democratic fund-raiser, Ed Pauley, as undersecretary of the Navy. Ickes publicly accused Pauley of trying to thwart the federal government's attempt to claim jurisdiction over California's oil-rich tidelands. Such a move, Pauley allegedly implied, would persuade oil companies to contribute to the Democratic Party in California. Ickes, always quick to be morally outraged, told a congressional committee that, in essence, Pauley was not fit to be undersecretary of the Navy.

Truman wanted Pauley in his "official family" and later wrote that FDR himself wanted Pauley in the job.[1] But Ickes portrayed himself as a crusader against what he called "government by crony."[2] If he intended to win the president's attention with that loaded phrase, he succeeded. A furious Truman told reporters that he supported Pauley despite Ickes' opposition. The secretary submitted his resignation, and the president eagerly—enthusiastically—accepted it. Ickes suggested that his resignation take effect in six weeks. "I wrote a brief note in reply," Truman recalled years later. "His resignation, I said, was accepted as of the following day."[3]

Harry Truman knew full well that with his political honeymoon long over, many critics now portrayed him as a small-time machine politician who stumbled into the presidency by accident. Truman certainly was loyal to his friends, including the Pendergasts, and appointed some to high positions, like Harry Vaughan who Truman named as his chief military aide because of their long ties dating back to World War I. Truman's crowd, critics said, were parochial and provincial, nothing like the bright, eager New Dealers who came to Washington with Roosevelt in 1933. Truman, for his part, was suspicious of the ideological New Dealers scattered by the thousands throughout Washington's bureaucracy. Truman biographer William E. Pemberton noted that the president "reacted strongly against eastern intellectuals with Ivy League backgrounds." He considered them to be "crackpot liberals."[4]

However, they too were Democrats, as Truman was, as the Pendergasts were. And if the party was to maintain its hold on Capitol Hill in 1946, the party would have to avoid the sort of backbiting and dissent that was breaking out in the Truman White House and among Democrats around the country.

The president seized an opportunity to speak to his fellow Democrats on March 23, when top party members gathered in the Mayflower Hotel near the White House for an annual tribute to President Andrew Jackson. Jackson Day dinners were an annual ritual for Democrats at the time, their equivalent of the Republican Party's annual Lincoln Day dinners held around the nation in mid-February. For Truman, the Jackson Day dinner offered a chance to rally his party and perhaps remind Democrats that the man they celebrated, Andrew Jackson, was not unlike their featured speaker. Jackson was the nation's first nonaristocratic president, a self-educated child of the Carolina backwoods who shocked the nation's gentry—and delighted his supporters—with his straightforward style and his skepticism of elites based in New England and Virginia. And, like the incumbent president, Jackson relied on a core group of friends, his "kitchen cabinet," for advice.

Before launching into his address, Truman greeted the nation's most prominent Democrats, including governors, members of Congress, and other officials. He posed for a picture with party chairman Robert Hannegan, a fellow Missouri Democrat who also served as postmaster general, and Secretary of Commerce Henry Wallace. The two men symbolized the party's cultural breach, with Hannegan representing the party's urban Catholic constituency and Wallace the progressive Protestant reform wing. It would be Truman's task to remind both men, and their constituencies, of their common ground as Democrats.

Truman began speaking at 10:15 p.m., after his listeners spent several hours feasting and drinking to Andrew Jackson's memory. But Truman reminded them of another Democrat whose memory they ought to treasure—his immediate predecessor. Although they were gathered to pay tribute to "a soldier of democracy—Andrew Jackson," Truman added that "recently there appeared another champion of social justice." Echoes of the man who had held the party together for so long prompted a great cheer. Were Roosevelt alive, Truman said, "he would bring us a challenge to improve the lot of mankind everywhere. He would say, 'fight on.'"

Truman's invocation of Roosevelt's memory was no accident. FDR presided over a disciplined, united party that led the country through Depression and war. Truman now had the task of maintaining that unity and purpose in peacetime. And, as everybody in that ballroom knew, this was no easy task. So he tried to remind them of the party's recent victories and of a philosophy that tied together Andrew Jackson and Franklin Roosevelt.

The Democrats, he said, were "determined to abolish the tragic inequities of the past. To hold our leadership, and the support of the American people, we must continually advance toward higher goals in keeping with our liberal heritage." Here, Truman defined the party's ideology, putting aside differences between Southern and Northern Democrats, between New Deal reformers and urban pragmatists. Whatever their disputes,

Democrats were united in "seeking to establish higher standards of living—a new health program, a new educational and social security program, an increased minimum wage, adequate housing, a further development of our natural resources, and, above all, a strong and progressive America now and for all time." This was, in essence, a pitch for his domestic agenda, an agenda which Republicans and Southern Democrats had thus far thwarted.

In addition to his proposed expansion of the New Deal, Truman emphasized the need for continued federal powers over wages and prices. Otherwise, he said, the nation might once again descend into depression. His administration's anti-inflation policies would, he said, stabilize the difficult transition from a wartime to a peacetime economy.

Managing that transition, however, would require more than executive fiat and congressional approval. Cooperation, he said, was vital—especially among Democrats.

"As in the nation at large," he said, speaking directly to his fellow party members, "there is diversity of opinion among us, but the fundamental principles of the Democratic Party bind us together in a unity of purpose—an inflexible determination that our party shall advance to new and greater achievements."

One goal worth achieving, he said, would be the construction of 2.7 million new homes by the end of 1947. It would be, he said, "the greatest home construction program in the history of this or any other country." Millions of soldiers were coming home. All would be able to capitalize on GI benefits to buy homes. The task of housing so many people in so short a time required unprecedented government involvement in the housing market—another expansion of federal power in the private economy. Truman sought to use federal powers to keep housing costs low so that veterans could take advantage of the benefits of the GI Bill, which made federal funds available for home mortgages.

More and more, Truman was showing that he intended to be more than an accidental president, more than a mere caretaker of his predecessor's policies. But he needed the approval of Congress, and he sensed that winning that approval would be difficult. "My friends in Congress have got to make a choice," he said, pointedly not singling out only Republicans. "They have got to make up their minds whether they are for veterans' rights, or whether they are going to bow to the real estate lobby."

He finished not with a partisan flourish, but with a call for all Americans to "continue to live courageously." Peace promised nothing save the absence of war—the nation faced new and daunting challenges at home and abroad.

Truman's fellow Democrats warmly applauded their president. But his words did not stem the tide of unrest and dissatisfaction in his party, and in the country.

Labor problems beset the nation in 1946. Mine workers union leader
John L. Lewis was a particular thorn in Truman's side.

CHAPTER 6

Government Seizure

Address to Congress
May 25, 1946

TRACK 6

HARRY TRUMAN CONSIDERED HIMSELF A FRIEND OF LABOR AND OFTEN CITED HIS support for prolabor legislation, including the National Labor Relations Act—better known as the Wagner Act. The NLRA guaranteed labor's right to organize and bargain collectively, a milestone in labor-management relations. Truman supported the bill with one of his first Senate votes in 1935.

His rhetoric, too, was prolabor. Truman's humble beginnings and his struggles to establish himself in the 1920s gave an edge to his Midwestern populist rhetoric. He was no more comfortable with eastern bankers and financiers than he was with the New Deal Ivy Leaguers he inherited from Franklin Roosevelt.

In the spring of 1946, however, Truman was preparing to confront several of the nation's largest unions. While the number of strikes and strikers decreased dramatically as winter ended, unrest in two vital industries—coal and railroads—threatened even greater disruptions in production. Truman believed that strikes in either industry would be disastrous for the economy and for the nation's standing in the postwar world. The president wanted to bring union leaders to the White House and tell them that his patience was gone. He vented in notes to himself: "Declare an emergency," he wrote, "call out troops. Start industry and put anyone to work who wants to go to work. If any [union] leader interferes, court martial him." He was particularly upset with the controversial head of the United Mine Workers union, John L. Lewis, who had led a strike during the war. Truman said of him, "Lewis ought to have been shot in 1942, but Franklin didn't have the guts to do it."[1]

As the threat of major strikes mounted, the public's mood soured. In less than a year, Truman seemed to have used up all of his political capital, all of the sympathy and good press he generated after taking over from Franklin Roosevelt in April 1945. His plain-speaking style, direct way of conducting business, and even his decidedly middle-class, Midwestern demeanor, celebrated a year earlier as a welcome contrast to his aristocratic, often-aloof predecessor, now seemed embarrassing. Journalists noted that Truman was finding new ways to alienate nearly every important constituency in Washington. "New Dealers are unhappy," reported the *New York Herald-Tribune*, "conservatives are critical, middle-of-the-roaders uncertain."[2]

It was around this time that the phrase, "to err is Truman," entered the American lexicon. The new-found contempt for the president was summed up by John L. Lewis. When Truman questioned the legality of a proposed new welfare fund for mine workers, Lewis snapped back: "What does Truman know about the legality of anything?"[3]

Management refused Lewis's demand for the welfare fund, to be paid for by a special levy on each ton of coal extracted from the earth and to be controlled by the union president. Truman considered the proposal to be "a new grab for more power on the part of the miners' boss."[4] Management clearly concurred, so on April 1, 1946, four hundred thousand miners walked off their jobs. It's hard to imagine, more than a half-century after the fact, how important coal was to the nation's overall economy. Steel, another vital industry, depended on coal for their furnaces. Consumers and businesses relied on coal for energy. The nation's auto industry was virtually shut down—General Motors was already paralyzed by the ongoing UAW strike, but without coal, Ford and Chrysler also ground to a halt. The president threw himself into efforts to bring the strike to a halt, bringing Lewis to the White House regularly for discussions, despite his distaste for the brash, divisive union leader.

Matters became unimaginably worse when the nation's railroad workers began to talk of a possible strike in May. Truman took a personal interest in this dispute even as he tried to resolve the mine strike. He managed to persuade eighteen of the industry's twenty unions to accept a raise of eighteen and a half cents per hour, but the two largest unions, both of them headed by allies of the president, held out for more. The head of the Brotherhood of Railroad Trainmen, A. F. Whitney, and the president of the Brotherhood of Locomotive Engineers, Alvanley Johnston, were politically savvy organizers who stepped in to help Truman win reelection to the Senate in 1940 when defeat seemed certain. They also rallied to his support in 1944, when Truman emerged as a possible vice-presidential candidate. To Truman's frustration, Johnston and Whitney continued to hold out, leading the president to order a postponement of any strike for sixty days while labor and management continued to negotiate.

The talks, however, went nowhere. Truman took the union's position to heart. The dispute, he believed, was no longer one between labor and management. It was between two union leaders and the United States government. During one testy negotiating session in the White House, Truman told the two men, "You are not going to tie up the country. If this is the way you want it, we'll stop you."[5]

With a second crippling strike on the horizon, John L. Lewis shrewdly made a bid for public support by announcing a twelve-day suspension of the mine strike, beginning May 13. Truman met with Lewis three days later, but the union leader had nothing new to say. Negotiations with management, he said, were going nowhere.

The nation's railroads were about to come to a screeching halt, with a strike deadline set for May 18. The impact on the nation's economy figured to be catastrophic—freight trains carried the bulk of the nation's goods, and passenger trains, in this age before air travel was common, provided vital links between the nation's cities.

Truman received a visit on May 17 from his erstwhile friends Whitney and Johnston, who explained that the strike would go forward as planned. Together, the men represented nearly three hundred thousand workers.

Truman was prepared for their response. On his desk was an executive order giving the United States government the power to seize control of the nation's railroads. "In the strike situation confronting us," the order read, "governmental seizure is imperative for the protection of the rights of our citizens."[6] The action was not unprecedented—Franklin Roosevelt had seized the nation's coal mines when Lewis led a strike in 1943. But FDR acted at the height of a war. Truman was prepared to seize private industry in a time of peace, although, as he and the country realized, this was hardly an ordinary peace.

Truman's actions had the desired effect, at least temporarily. The union leaders agreed to put off their strike until five o'clock on May 23—a five-day respite. A confident Truman told a news conference that the postponement meant that the workers would not, in the end, go on strike.

After just forty-eight hours, however, it became clear that Truman's confidence was misplaced. Negotiations were deadlocked, as were talks aimed at resolving the miners' strike. On Wednesday, May 22, Truman and the country faced the prospect of massive strikes in two of the nation's most important industries, coal (where Lewis's twelve-day truce was nearing its expiration date) and the railroads.

The president ordered government seizure of the coal mines on May 22. The following day, the railroad union leaders visited the White House, where they were presented with Truman's compromise plan for a pay raise of eighteen and a half cents per hour. They rejected it immediately. According to Truman biographer David McCullough, presidential advisor John Steelman was astonished, telling Whitney and Johnston that nobody ought to refuse a request from the president of the United States. According to McCullough, the leaders replied by saying that "nobody paid attention to this president anyway."[7] For Harry Truman, increasingly embattled and frustrated, those sentiments were the equivalent of a declaration of war.

The strike commenced at five o'clock on May 23. All over the country, passenger and freight trains simply stopped running. Commuters were left to their own devices as they were ordered off trains in stations miles away from their destination. Delivery of every sort of consumer and industrial product was put on hold indefinitely, including food and gasoline.

Truman, furious over what he saw as the union leaders' selfish, unpatriotic attitude, put his thoughts on paper. The result was what David McCullough called "one of the most intemperate documents ever written by an American president."[8] Intended as a speech to be delivered to the nation, Truman asked veterans to help him "eliminate" people like Lewis, Whitney, and Johnston, among others. He lashed out at all workers on strike, saying that they were "living in luxury, working when they pleased." He charged that railroad workers made forty times the salary of a combat soldier. None of it was true.

Fortunately, Truman did not deliver this speech. Press secretary Charlie Ross, an old friend from Missouri, persuaded him that it was too divisive and simply not presidential. But Truman was determined to say, and do, something. He told his advisors that he intended to speak to the nation that night, May 24, and to Congress the following day. He said he intended to use his power as commander in chief to draft the striking workers into the Army, forcing them back on the job. The job of rewriting—and toning down—the president's remarks was handed to Ross, Samuel Rosenman, and Clark Clifford, a new face in the Truman White House. They chose to delete mention of drafting railroad workers, but the speech declared that the administration would move ahead with its plan to seize the railroads if workers did not return to their jobs by 4:00 p.m. the following day.

At 10:00 p.m. Washington time, Truman addressed the nation by radio, saying that Americans faced a crisis on the magnitude of the Japanese attack on Pearl Harbor in 1941. He pointedly singled out Whitney and Johnston, accusing them of deliberately causing havoc and suffering throughout the world, for without railroads, he said, American food shipments to Europe were disrupted. Starvation and death would follow, and Whitney and Johnston were to blame, he said.

At four o'clock the following afternoon, as workers ignored Truman's deadline to return to work, a somber Harry Truman entered the House of Representatives to speak to a joint session of Congress about his plan to seize the railroads and to bring about an end to the great wave of strikes and unrest. He received a rousing ovation as he entered, but he did not acknowledge the show of support. There were no smiles, no friendly gestures. Harry Truman was ready to go to war.

He began with a frightening scenario: the railroad strike, he said, would lead not just to higher prices and inconvenience. It would result in mass starvation in Europe and Asia, where war refugees depended on timely shipments of food from America. Because of the stakes involved, he announced that the U.S. Army would take over operation of the railroads.

"This is no longer a dispute between labor and management," he said. "It has now become a strike against the government of the United States itself. That kind of strike can never be tolerated. If allowed to continue, the government will break down. Strikes against the government must stop."

He conceded that some members of Congress no doubt believed he should have taken strong action sooner, but he thought patience would be rewarded with a fair settlement. Blocking that settlement, and thwarting his patient approach, were two men. Again, he singled out his former allies Johnston and Whitney for bitter, withering criticism.

"This particular crisis has been brought about by the obstinate arrogance of two men," he said. "They are Mr. Alvanley Johnston, President of the Brotherhood of Locomotive Engineers, and Mr. A. F. Whitney, President of the Brotherhood of Railway Trainmen. Eighteen other unions and all of the railroad companies of the nation are ready to run the railroads, and these two men have tried to stop them." It would be tempting, he said, for Congress to "seek vengeance" against the duo for their "unpatriotic act." But, he added, "I am sure that none of us wishes to take any action which will injure labor. The contribution of labor to the growth of this country in peace and to victory in war, is at least as great as that of any other group in our population. Without well-paid, well-housed, and well-nourished working men and women in this country, it would stagnate and decay."

Truman said he wanted an end to the crisis, but he sought no campaign against organized labor. The fault was not with the movement, but with "a handful of men who are striking against their own Government and against every one of their fellow citizens—and against themselves."

Beyond the immediate crisis, Truman asked Congress to consider measures that would bring about some amount of peace to the workplace so that the process of reconversion at home and reconstruction abroad could continue without interruption.

"As a part of this temporary emergency legislation," he said, "I request the Congress immediately to authorize the president to draft into the Armed Forces of the United States all workers who are on strike against their Government." The startling request, which even some of his own aides opposed, led senators and congressmen to howl with delight. Harry Truman was not the only politician in town tired of labor disputes and strikes.

As the applause died down and Truman continued to give away nothing in his expression, a Senate staff member approached the podium and handed Truman a note. He paused in his delivery, which surely must have puzzled the millions listening on radio. Then, without a smile or even a hint of satisfaction, he revealed the note's contents: the villains of his speech, Whitney and Johnston, had just told White House aides that they would abide by the president's wage offer and would return to work. "Word has just been received," he said, "that the railroad strike has been settled, on terms proposed by the president."

The chamber burst into even wilder applause. For the moment, everybody was wild about Harry. He had beaten the unions, but the president chose not to gloat. Instead, he continued to read from a speech that remained relevant, laying out other measures designed to prevent what everybody feared—the onset of another economic depression. He urged Congress to take steps to stabilize prices and increase production, while also maintaining the right of unions to strike. "The whole subject of labor relations should be studied afresh," he said, urging Congress to create a commission to study the issue.

Congress signaled its approval, not so much for the president's specific recommendations but for the drama of the afternoon and the successful conclusion to the potentially catastrophic strike. But his proposal to draft striking workers failed in the Senate after winning overwhelming passage in the House of Representatives. Many aging New Dealers, including union leader Sidney Hillman, found Truman's proposal appalling, a sign that Franklin Roosevelt's successor was not a real New Dealer after all.

Truman, however, was unaffected by what his critics said. He was, he said, the "servant of 150 million people of the United States, and I had to do the job even if I lost my political career."[9]

Before long, such a scenario seemed increasingly likely. Truman's stand against the railroad workers won him only a respite, not a moratorium, from public criticism.

Henry Wallace was an original New Dealer and the man Truman replaced on the national ticket as vice president in 1944. Wallace left Truman's cabinet and wound up running against him in 1948.

CHAPTER 7

Out of Control

Radio Address on Lifting
Price Controls on Meat
October 14, 1946

TRACK 7

F OR HARRY TRUMAN, 1946 WAS A SUMMER OF EXTREME DISCONTENT. HIS SPIKE in public acclaim was short-lived as the railroad crisis faded from memory. Bread-and-butter issues continued to vex him, as did foreign affairs and even his personnel decisions.

His biggest concern at home was the possible return to Depression-like conditions as millions of servicemen and women returned home, looking for a place in the work force. He, and many others, feared a combination of high unemployment and out-of-control inflation as wartime price controls came up for debate on Capitol Hill. While labor's militancy waned after Truman's decisive action against the railroad workers, peace on the home front was brittle and, in some cases, begrudging. Few would argue that the unions had been tamed, or that management was more conciliatory toward workers. Another round of strikes could break out at any minute, and many in government feared they would.

There was turbulence within his inner circle, leading the press to conclude that Truman's show of strength against the railroad workers may have been a mirage. He seemed incapable of handling his own cabinet, never mind the country. Impressions that Truman was in over his head grew over the summer, and Republicans, with their eyes set on winning control of

Congress in November, were eager to foster them. They coined the phrase, "to err is Truman."

There was no lack of material to justify the jest. Building on Harold Ickes's complaint that the administration was run by cronies of the president—rather than supposedly disinterested experts like himself and other New Dealers—the press and Republicans assailed Truman's appointment of John Snyder, a banker from St. Louis, as treasury secretary. Snyder was not particularly charismatic. He shared the president's taste for bourbon, and exuded Main Street, not Wall Street. But he had one important virtue: the president had known him for years and trusted him. "My selection of Snyder," Truman later wrote, "was based on a long association which had existed between us."[1] But for many, that was hardly a recommendation for such an important post as secretary of the treasury.

The press, encouraged by disgruntled holdovers from the New Deal years, continued to portray the Truman White House as a band of mediocrities. As historian Donald R. McCoy wrote in his study of the Truman years, the press was filled with stories "about Truman and his cronies" whose "jests and pranks...too often made the White House sound like an American Legion hall."[2] Public impressions of more vaunted Truman aides were not much better, as the press followed reports of infighting among top aides, including Secretary of State James Byrnes, Commerce Secretary Henry Wallace, and Navy Secretary James Forrestal.

Truman's popularity rating dropped from more than 80 percent in early 1946 to just over 50 percent by summertime. And yet, the nation's worst fears about the economy had not come to pass on Truman's watch. There was no return to breadlines, mass unemployment, and fear itself. Veterans were absorbed into the workforce, as many of the millions of women who were the backbone of American output during the war left the factory floor to return to domestic life. The jobless rate was less than 4 percent, and with inflation seemingly under control, American purchasing power continued to increase. Cutbacks in government spending for war material did not lead to a catastrophic drop in production. In short, reconversion to a peacetime economy, while painful, was proceeding about as well as could be expected. The federal budget for fiscal year 1947 (which began in the summer of 1946) was balanced, and would show a surplus over the next several years.

The man in charge, however, was more likely to be blamed for the pain than given credit for good news. Republicans on Capitol Hill, out of power for a decade and a half, were delighted to turn the impending congressional elections into a referendum on Truman's performance.

Conflict between Truman and Congress came to a head in late June, when Capitol Hill sent Truman a bill designed to extend wartime controls on prices, loaded with exemptions for certain industries. Truman had been asking Congress for an extension of price controls for months, knowing that the wartime measure was due to expire on June 30. Congress finally acted in late June, sending a bill to Truman on June 29, a day before the old law expired. Although the bill gave the president power to regulate prices in general, it contained an amendment allowing manufacturers to receive the same profits they received on their goods in 1941, when profit margins were high. The amendment, offered by Republican Senator Robert Taft of Ohio, also allowed manufacturers to increase prices to account for increases in costs since 1941.

Furious, Truman angrily vetoed the bill. In a radio address to the nation, he said the measure "was no price control bill at all." Had he signed it, he said, "I would have encouraged the false impression that you were going to be protected for the next year from excessive price increases."[3] In his veto message to Congress, Truman wrote that "inflation has already gutted the economy of country after country all over the world."[4] It would happen in the United States, he said, if government were stripped of the power to act.

Congress revisited the issue two weeks later, but the new bill continued to exempt some commodities, including meat, from price controls. A further provision forbade any attempt to reimpose controls on meat until August 20. Truman reluctantly signed the bill, believing Congress would do no better. Almost immediately, the price of livestock skyrocketed, and cattlemen quickly brought their animals to slaughterhouses, looking to cash in on higher prices. Once again, events seemed out of the president's control as the slaughter of the summer of 1946 gave way to a severe meat shortage in the early fall, when price controls were reimposed and cattle-owners stopped bringing livestock to market.

In the middle of yet another domestic crisis, Truman found himself embroiled in controversy over a speech given in New York by his commerce secretary, Henry Wallace. The former vice president—the man who was removed from FDR's ticket in favor of Truman in 1944—told members of the leftist Congress of Industrial Unions that the United States should resist the urge to confront the Soviet Union over its dominance of Eastern Europe. Imperialism, he said, posed a far greater danger of renewed war than Communism did, an assertion that suggested American allies such as Britain and France were more likely to start a war than the Soviet Union. The mostly pro-Soviet audience cheered the speech. When Truman was asked about it, he told reporters that he had approved the speech and that it reflected his administration's policy. That came as news to Secretary of State Byrnes, who was in Paris negotiating with the Soviets over the future of Germany and other difficult issues. Byrnes, like nearly all of Truman's foreign-policy advisors, believed that negotiating with the Soviets required strong words, not friendly platitudes.

The clear divergence between Wallace—who, as commerce secretary, had no standing to deliver foreign-policy pronouncements—and Byrnes made it seem as though Truman either didn't understand Wallace's assertions or simply wasn't minding his administrative store. Either way, the president looked weak and anything but in charge of his own cabinet and policy. He tried to recover by saying that he approved of Wallace's right to deliver such a speech, not the sentiments he expressed. The president liked Wallace and understood his symbolic importance—Henry Wallace was the last New Dealer, the last member of FDR's original cabinet still in office. He was the favorite son of the party's left wing, an important constituency for any Democratic president. Truman kept Wallace in the cabinet, even after newspapers got hold of a letter the secretary had written in which he asserted that some American military commanders wanted to attack the Soviet Union. The ensuing uproar did nothing to change the public's disenchantment with Truman and his apparent inability to keep his cabinet, never mind the country, running smoothly.

On September 18, 1946, Truman wrote about the Wallace controversy in a letter to his mother and sister. "I think he'll quit today and I won't shed any tears," the president wrote. "Never was there such a mess and it is partly my making. But when I make a mistake it is a good one."[5] The president was wrong. Wallace didn't quit. Truman fired him two days later, on September 20. He wrote again to his mother and sister, "So—this morning I called Henry and told him he'd better get out and he was so nice about it I almost backed out!" The party's liberals and old New Dealers assailed the president, but he pretended not to care. He wrote, "The crackpots are having conniption fits. I'm glad they are. It convinces me I'm right."[6]

The country, however, was not so sure that anything Harry Truman did was right. With the congressional election just weeks away, American consumers found the meat counters in their local grocery stores empty more often than not. The rush to slaughter in the summer meant that fewer animals were available for market, and with the reimposition of price controls on meat, livestock owners were in no hurry to bring cows, pigs, chicken, and other animals to market. Speaker Sam Rayburn, a Texas Democrat, saw disaster looming in November. "This is going to be a damned beefsteak election," he said. If so, Democrats would be reduced to chopped meat in November.[7]

Political aides urged Truman to accept the inevitable, and perhaps retain a few Congressional seats, by ending price controls on meat. Such a measure would increase supply and end the shortage, hopefully in time for Election Day. Truman hated the idea. He was furious with "a reckless group of selfish men—some of them inside the Congress, some outside—who were encouraging sellers to gamble on the destruction of price control."[8]

On October 14, a reluctant president addressed the nation to announce that he would end price controls on meat. He acknowledged the "hardship" that his listeners were suffering "because of the lack of meat."

"I sympathize with the millions of housewives who have been hard-pressed to provide nourishing meals for their families," he said. "I sympathize particularly with our thousands of veterans and other patients in hospitals throughout the country. I know that our children, as well as those persons engaged in manual labor, need meat in their diet."

The issue of shortages, especially of a staple like meat, seemed incomprehensible in the midst of plenty, and infuriating after so much sacrifice during the war. Americans, Truman understood, had good reason to be angry over meat shortages caused not by a lack of purchasing power, but by economic forces and political maneuvering.

"Many of us," he said, "have asked the same questions: Why should there be a meat shortage when there are millions of cattle and hogs on the ranges and farms and in feed lots in this country? Who are the persons responsible for this serious condition? Why doesn't the Government do something about it?" The answer, he said, was simple: Congress was to blame.

"The responsibility rests squarely on a few men in the Congress who, in the service of selfish interests, have been determined for some time to wreck price controls no matter what the cost might be to our people," he said.

Truman was a feisty character who rarely backed down from a fight and he resented Senator Robert Taft's efforts to undo price controls within a bill that was designed to continue the regulations. Now, with the nation listening, he sought to place blame for meat shortages squarely on the shoulders of his former colleagues on Capitol Hill. And not just Republicans. Truman was as angry with many Democrats as he was with Republicans. In another draft of this speech, he said that members of Congress had "deserted your president for a mess of pottage, a piece of beef, a side of bacon." Although he didn't single out Democrats for criticism, his target was clear. He accused these unnamed critics of forgetting the work of Franklin Roosevelt. "You've gone over to the powers of selfishness and greed," he wrote.[9] He never delivered this speech. But the speech he gave certainly reflected his feelings.

He told Americans that "selfish men" had rushed their cattle to market before prices were reregulated in August. The mass slaughter of the summer was carried out to maximize profits without regard to the nation's well-being. Now, with Republicans in Congress promising to end price controls in January, cattle-owners were withholding their products, waiting for a chance to make further profits. Americans, he said, would not "condone the conduct of those who, in order further to fatten their profits, are endangering the health of our people by holding back vital foods which are now ready for market and for which the American people are clamoring." Those people who acted in such a calculating fashion, he said, were the same who "hated Franklin D. Roosevelt and fought everything he stood for. This same group did its best to discredit his efforts to achieve a better life for our people." With Democrats frantically trying to hold onto Congress, and Truman trying to avoid political embarrassment, the president conjured the ghost of Franklin Roosevelt in an effort to rally Americans behind his administration.

Truman vented again as he explained that he had given "long and serious consideration" to seizing privately owned cattle and sending them to slaughterhouses to relieve the meat shortage. He decided, however, that the nation's cattle simply were spread too far across the land for such a plan to work. That he would even consider such a measure, however, spoke to his frustration.

"There is only one remedy left," he said, with a sense of resignation in his voice. "That is to lift controls on meat. Accordingly, the secretary of agriculture and the price administrator are removing all price controls on livestock, and food and feed products therefrom—tomorrow."

Truman made a point of reminding listeners that the meat industry insisted that price decontrol would end the shortage. "The American people," he said, "will know where the responsibility rests if profiteering on meat raises prices so high that the average American cannot buy it." It would not be Harry Truman's fault.

The meat crisis, just one of so many in the first full year of peace since 1940, finally did come to an end. But Americans were not inclined to blame "selfish men" for the shortage. Their fingers pointed directly toward the White House.

President Truman and Bess greet
UN delegates from around the world.

CHAPTER 8

The End of Isolation

Speech to the United Nations
General Assembly
October 23, 1946

TRACK 8

ARRY TRUMAN'S FELLOW DEMOCRATS COULD FEEL THE POLITICAL PLATES shifting under their feet in the fall of 1946. The president's popularity continued its inexorable decline, bottoming out at a 32 percent approval rating in October. He could do nothing right, it seemed. Qualities that seemed like virtues only a year earlier—the president's candor, his everyman persona, his modesty, his loyalty to friends—were now dreadful liabilities. Eastern establishment types from both parties cringed when they heard Truman's flat Midwestern accent, or saw pictures of him with his Missouri friends. He was scorned even for his devotion to his elderly mother, whose health was becoming precarious.

Harry Truman became a political lightning rod as the nation prepared for its first peacetime congressional elections since 1940. Democrats avoided any mention of their presumed standard-bearer; Republicans, on the other hand, tried to turn every Democrat into a presidential crony. Few would have predicted such a turn of events in the summer of 1945, when a confident nation accepted the surrender of its enemies and set about reconstructing the world in its image. Peacetime, however, brought not just glory but challenges that tested the nation's patience. Americans seemed inclined to blame Harry Truman for failing to somehow banish the complaints of organized labor, the shortages of meat and other commodities, and the general malaise that accompanied the war's end.

While domestic issues dominated the concerns of many Americans as the election approached, the politics of the postwar world also factored in the nation's collective disillusion. Peace and victory certainly did not bring a return to what Warren Harding called, after another world war, "normalcy." But Americans had been warned for years that there would be no return to isolationism this time. Franklin Roosevelt made the point in several of his wartime fireside chats—without a firm American presence in the postwar world, he said, no genuine peace would follow the war. He did not say, however, that with leadership came not just the privileges of the powerful, but the burdens of decision makers.

The Soviet Union's behavior and ambitions were the chief cause of American anxiety across the globe. The wartime alliance showed cracks even while Roosevelt was alive, but relations declined quickly as the war came to an end and the victors studied maps of the postwar world. As early as February 1946, it became clear that the end of combat hostilities across the globe would not bring an end to tensions and profound disagreements among the victors. Joseph Stalin gave an inflammatory speech on February 9 in which he asserted, in essence, that capitalism was the root cause of global conflict, past, present, and future. The Soviets, he said, would carry out a massive effort to defend themselves against an inevitable challenge from Western capitalist nations, including, by implication, his recent allies, the United States and Great Britain. American policymakers saw Stalin's speech as a cover for expansionist policies in Eastern Europe and elsewhere. Weeks later, a young American diplomat in Moscow named George Kennan wrote a long telegram to Secretary of States James Byrnes, suggesting that the U.S. and its allies work to contain Soviet influence in the world. The Soviets, he said, were acting out Russia's traditional insecurities and neuroses regarding the West. There was little use trying to engage Stalin, Kennan argued, who capitalized on the hostility of other nations to justify his own brutal rule at home.

Kennan's telegram made the rounds of official Washington just as the Soviets were attempting to extend their influence in Turkey, Iran, and Korea. Winston Churchill, now the leader of the opposition in Britain's House of Commons, arrived in the United States in early March, intent on adding his view to the ongoing debate over how to deal with Stalin and the Soviets. Churchill and the president traveled by train from Washington to Fulton, Missouri, where the former prime minister was due to deliver a foreign policy speech at Westminster College. Truman, perhaps understanding that any attempt at Churchillian eloquence was doomed to failure, introduced the former prime minister with a quick anecdote and then turned the stage over to the more accomplished orator. The Cold War was about to become a good deal warmer as Churchill delivered what he would later argue was an appeal for peace. He was not wrong, if one read the speech in its entirety. But the speech became famous for one characteristically bellicose flourish. "From Stettin in the Baltic to Trieste in the Adriatic," he said, "an iron curtain has descended across the Continent. Behind that line lie all the capitals of the ancient states of central and eastern Europe. Warsaw, Berlin, Prague, Vienna, Budapest, Belgrade, Bucharest, and Sofia, all these famous cities and the populations around them lie in what I must call the Soviet sphere..." He went on to propose an alliance among the Western democracies, particularly one between the United States and the United Kingdom, to defend against Soviet expansionism.

The speech, not surprisingly, created an uproar. Truman saw it beforehand and approved, although he pointed out that it was certain to create controversy, and so it did. Truman appeared surprised when commentators on both sides of the Atlantic condemned Churchill, so recently a global hero, for making a bad situation even worse. The president neither rallied behind a suddenly embattled Churchill, nor did he put any distance between the Briton's words and his own policies. He tried to explain away the controversy to Stalin, offering the Soviet leader his own soapbox in the United States if he wished to respond to Churchill. Stalin refused.

Once again, it appeared as though Truman was in over his head, too small for a job that required intellectual finesse and agility. The subsequent crises of the summer, both at home and abroad, did nothing to change that perception. Historians of the Cold War note that whatever Truman really thought of Churchill's Iron Curtain speech, his administration became increasingly more hostile to the Soviets as 1946 progressed, leading to Henry Wallace's criticisms and his resignation in the fall. Ironically, Republicans, including a young congressman from California named Richard Nixon, seemed to think that the administration was coddling the Soviets. Nixon and others began to assert a charge that would become increasingly loud and shrill in coming years—Democrats, they said, were too soft on the threat of Communist expansion abroad and subversion at home.

As the public turned against him, and his fellow Democrats pretended he didn't exist, Truman seemed unchanged, at least in public. But he was frustrated and disappointed, as a diary entry from September 26, 1946, indicated. The date was an important one for Harry Truman—it was the anniversary of the beginning of the Battle of Argonne Forest during World War I. Captain Harry Truman and his men in Battery B, 2nd Battalion, 129th Field Artillery, opened fire before dawn on the morning of September 26, 1918, pouring round after round at hidden German positions. Later that day, Truman and his men moved forward into a smoldering, scarred landscape as the enemy poured on fire of its own. It was a harrowing, unforgettable experience, one that moved Truman to reflection as he sat in the White House as commander in chief nearly thirty years later.

Referring to himself in the third person as "my acquaintance," he wrote of how he was treated as a hero when he turned home from war, only to see how quickly "people forgot the war." Before long, they voted against Woodrow Wilson's Democrats, who presided over the war effort, and decided to turn "the clock back."[1]

For Truman, the comparison was clear. Americans were happy when the latest world war ended, just as they were happy in 1918. "Then," he wrote, "the reaction set in. Selfishness, greed, jealousy raised their ugly heads. No wartime incentive to keep them down. Labor began to grab all it could get by fair means or foul, farmers began black-marketing food, industry hoarded inventories, and the same old pacifists began to talk disarmament. But my acquaintance tried to meet every situation and has met them up to now. Can he continue to outface the demagogues, the chiselers, the jealousies?"

He insisted that he could. But by even raising the issue, Harry Truman seemed to admit more than a little doubt—about himself, and his fellow citizens.

Although he agreed to keep a low public profile in the weeks leading to November's off-year elections, Truman was determined to play a role in supporting and encouraging the fledgling United Nations organization, an institution he believed might yet prevent the repeat of mistakes that followed World War I. On October 23, 1946, the president and his wife Bess flew to New York to attend the opening of the United Nations General Assembly on the old World's Fair grounds in the Flushing Meadows section of Queens (the permanent UN headquarters in Manhattan would not be completed until 1952). Truman believed his presence would send a strong message to the international community that the United States was committed to world leadership and collective security, that it would not make the mistake it made after World War I.

In a welcoming speech to delegates gathered in the former New York State pavilion in the fairgrounds, the president took note of the change in official U.S. attitudes toward global institutions. "For the people of my country," he said, "this meeting today has a special historic significance. After the First World War the United States refused to join the League of Nations and our seat was empty at the first meeting of the League assembly. This time the United States is not only a member; it is the host to the United Nations...This meeting of the Assembly symbolizes the abandonment by the United States of a policy of isolation."

Truman's remarks certainly were welcome in the large hall that served as the General Assembly's temporary meeting place, but they were not without a sharp edge. At home, a revived Republican Party—the traditional voice of American isolationism—was poised to take over Congress, with unknowable implications for the conduct of U.S. foreign policy. While few Republican leaders actively opposed UN membership, Truman did not underestimate the power of isolationist voices in American culture. "In foreign affairs the Republican leadership was still suffering from the aftereffects of isolationism," Truman later wrote.[2] In his speech, he told delegates that the "overwhelming majority of the American people, regardless of party, support the United Nations." These were happy words, indeed, for the world's diplomats.

Truman did not evade the major international problem that overshadowed nearly every other postwar issue, from reconstruction to repatriation: the profound disagreements between the war's victors over construction of a new world order. "I must tell you," he said, "that the American people are troubled by the failure of the Allied nations to make more progress in their common search for a lasting peace." But the fault, he said, was not that of the UN, but of the allies themselves. The UN was not founded to sort victor from vanquished or to preside over the details of a postwar settlement. That task, he said, was up to the Allies themselves. The UN would be charged with the responsibility of maintaining international peace after, not before, the Allies negotiated a final peace settlement.

Using a formula that his predecessor famously articulated before the United States entered World War II, Truman said the postwar world must be governed by "four essential freedoms," which were, "freedom of speech, freedom of religion, freedom from want, and freedom from fear." Truman did not need to remind his listeners that Franklin Roosevelt devised the Four Freedoms formula as a basis for lasting peace. But he did remind them that the time to implement the formula was upon them. "We shall attain freedom from fear when every act of every nation, in its dealings with every other nation, brings closer to realization the other freedoms—freedom of speech, freedom of religion, and freedom from want. Along this path we can find justice for all, without distinction between the strong and the weak among nations, and without discrimination among individuals."

Truman again acknowledged that the Allies remained at odds over the postwar settlement. But, in a conciliatory gesture, he told delegates that it would be a mistake to exaggerate the differences between the West and the Soviet Union. "Above all," he said, "we must not permit differences in economic and social systems to stand in the way of peace, either now or in the future." His words were intended more for his negotiating partners than the delegates seated in front of him, for he asserted that the UN could not begin its work until the Allies "reach agreement on the peace settlements."

That task, in Truman's view, could be achieved only if the nations of the world pledged themselves to ensuring freedom from want. Want and fear were related; freedom from the former would help ensure freedom from the latter. "The United Nations will not be able to remove the fear of war from the world unless substantial progress can be made in the next few years toward the realization of another of the four freedoms—freedom from want." The president praised various UN agencies and other international organizations for their efforts to bring the promise of a decent life to all nations.

Truman's speech and his very presence at the General Assembly's opening ensured a strong U.S. presence at the UN. Truman was a true believer in the organization's potential to relieve human suffering and mediate human conflict. After his speech, he and Bess greeted delegates at a reception in the pavilion's lobby. Mrs. Truman was not fond of the public eye and formal political affairs, but she gamely stood to her husband's right as they shook hands with dozens of strangers. A bright corsage may have lifted her spirits as she and her husband pumped the hands of strangers, some of them, like the Saudi delegates, dressed in exotic clothing. Young military officers, unsmiling, watched over the proceedings until the last hand was shaken, the last photo taken. Then, the president and his wife were driven to Manhattan for another reception at the Waldorf Astoria, followed by a long trip by rail back to Washington later that night.

The nation went to the polls on November 2, less than two weeks after Truman's appearance at the United Nations. Truman's Democrats were pummeled in a historic landslide. They lost fifty-four seats in the House of Representatives and twelve seats in the Senate. Republicans would control the new Eightieth Congress for the first time since the Hoover administration.

Truman's party, his friends, and his family were upset. The president kept his thoughts to himself, except for something he told his daughter, Margaret, as the bad news poured in on election night. "Don't worry," he said, "I know how things will turn out and they'll be all right."[3]

PART TWO:
Comeback, 1947–1948

Harry Truman with his family and Cabinet as they prepare to go
to Capitol Hill for the 1948 State of the Union address.

Introduction

THE DEMOCRATIC DEFEATS IN CONGRESS IN 1946 SEEMED TO SIGNAL AN END TO the era that began with Franklin Roosevelt's inauguration in March 1933. The nation turned away from the politics and policies that led to four straight decisive victories in presidential elections, responding to Republican candidates who capitalized on voter dissatisfaction with the status quo. Harry Truman basked in the glow of victory in 1945, but within months of the German and Japanese surrenders, Americans seemed to forget their sense of joy and relief over the war's end. Strikes and shortages dominated domestic politics, and increased tensions with the Soviet Union signaled the beginning of a global ideological conflict. Harry Truman seemed to shrink in stature in 1946, and Republicans were delighted to run against him in the midterm elections. The strategy worked.

When the new Congress met in January 1947, Harry Truman faced something Franklin Roosevelt never did—a hostile Senate and House determined to make life difficult for the sitting president. But something unexpected began to unfold through 1947 and into 1948. President Truman took the political fight to Capitol Hill, challenging Republicans to live up to their promises. He struck a balance with allies in the labor movement, denouncing John L. Lewis of the United Mine Workers but also vetoing the Taft-Hartley Act, designed to reign in labor's right to organize and strike.

Globally, Truman implemented one of the most important initiatives of his presidency, a plan to rebuild Europe named for his secretary of state, George C. Marshall. The president also promised to assist nations trying to resist Communist aggression, a stance that became known as the Truman Doctrine.

Still, as the 1948 election approached, Truman seemed a sure loser. Some Democrats, including President Roosevelt's son James, desperately sought to dump Truman as the party's candidate. Truman was nominated anyway, but Southern Democrats nominated a third-party candidate, Strom Thurmond, and some liberals supported former vice president Henry Wallace, another third-party candidate.

Undaunted, Harry Truman ran a campaign for the ages. When the votes were counted on election night, he was elected president in his own right. He also became a political legend.

CHAPTER 9

The Real Truman Administration

State of the Union Speech
January 6, 1947

TRACK 9

A T TEN THIRTY ON THE MORNING OF NEW YEAR'S EVE, 1946, HARRY TRUMAN invited reporters into the Oval Office for a special announcement. The reporters, who were meeting with Truman for the 93rd time in his short presidency, must have felt as though they had been transported back in time. For on this last day of 1946, some sixteen months after V-J Day, Harry Truman read a proclamation declaring that hostilities associated with World War II would come to an end at noontime.

The proclamation was a legalism, a document designed to bring to an end many of the powers Washington assumed during the war, including the right to seize war-related industries threatened by strikes or other interruptions. Truman said the proclamation covered fifty-three laws designed to last only until the president declared an end to hostilities. Twenty expired immediately; the others expired within six months of Truman's proclamation.

The president noted that the proclamation did not mean that the war was over, at least not officially, and that the national emergency requested by Franklin Roosevelt in 1939 remained in place. The reporters seemed confused until Truman reminded them that only Congress could declare an end to the war—just as only Congress could declare war—and only Congress could reverse a national emergency declared through legislation.

His New Year's Eve proclamation, he explained, "terminates the period of hostilities and terminates the fifty-three laws which are affected specifically by the Congress."[1]

One reporter thought he detected a political motivation in the formal announcement. Congress, after all, had been agitating for just such a proclamation in order to further remove wartime restrictions on the economy. "Mr. President," the reporter asked, "is this the beginning of your cooperation with the new Congress? They have been trying to do this—they have been talking about it."

Truman offered a conciliatory answer. "Well, yes," he said, "this is in cooperation with the Congress."

The electoral disaster of early November did not appear to discourage Truman. Rather, he seemed reinvigorated, almost spoiling for the legislative fight he knew would come sooner rather than later. The Democratic Party's overwhelming losses were a milestone, the end of an era that began with Democratic victories in the 1930 congressional elections a year into the Great Depression. The old era belonged to Franklin Roosevelt. The new era was Harry Truman's.

His friends and aides noticed the unexpected change in Truman's demeanor. Press aide Charlie Ross wrote that the president acted like a "free man."

"The real Truman administration," Ross said, "began the day after the elections."[2]

Truman's critics might have argued the same point, but without Ross's implicit optimism. Indeed, one prominent Democrat was so fearful of a "real" Truman administration that he sought to prevent it. Senator William Fulbright of Arkansas publicly proposed that Truman appoint Republican Senator Arthur Vandenberg—one of Truman's favorite Republicans and a bipartisan consensus seeker—as secretary of state, replacing James Byrnes. After making the appointment, Fulbright suggested, Truman should then resign, allowing Vandenberg to become president—at the time, the vice-presidency was vacant, so, according to the Presidential Succession Act of 1886, the secretary of state was next in line. The Fulbright plan was taken seriously enough that Ross had to assure reporters that Truman had no intention of quitting. Truman's daughter, Margaret, wrote that "Dad ignored this bit of idiocy."[3] He may have ignored it, but he certainly didn't forget it. From then on, Truman referred to the senator from Arkansas as "half-bright."

From Truman's perspective, the November elections were not quite the catastrophe many others believed they were. In a letter to his mother and sister, Truman cited a note he received from Eleanor Roosevelt, his predecessor's widow, in mid-November. The former first lady told him, he wrote, that "I would have no more—and maybe not as much trouble with the Congress coming up than I had with the supposedly Democratic Congress I had had for the last two years. She may be right."[4]

As Republicans celebrated and Democrats wrung their hands in late 1946, Harry Truman seized an opportunity to remind all concerned that he was still president of the United States—to the apparent chagrin of Senator Fulbright—and that he had no intention of simply minding the store for the remainder of his term. His old antagonist John L. Lewis, head of the mine workers union, took advantage of Truman's perceived weakness after the congressional elections by threatening a massive, nationwide strike on the eve of the winter heating season. Harry Truman was ready, willing, and—to the apparent surprise of Lewis—able to respond to the UMW's illegal action. The coal mines were still under government seizure, which allowed the Truman administration to argue in court that a strike would violate the Smith-Connally Act—the very law which Truman would dispose of in just a matter of weeks. Smith-Connally forbade strikes against facilities and industries under government control. The courts agreed, handing down a temporary injunction barring a strike. The miners responded by walking off the job anyway.

Their actions played into Harry Truman's hands. In early December, a federal judge fined the union $3 million for its actions. Lewis himself was hit with a $10,000 fine on contempt of court charges. Faced with these enormous sanctions and public outrage, the workers returned to the mines on December 7. Harry Truman had himself an enormous and popular victory only four weeks after the country seemed to reject his agenda and leadership.

So it was a confident Truman, not a chastened Truman, who prepared for the new year and the new Republican-led Congress. He did not need a reminder that 1947 would set the stage for the following year's presidential election, when he would run for a full term in his own right. Republicans were certain to use their new power on Capitol Hill to push their own agenda while blocking his—such was the nature of politics, as Truman knew well.

But the president had a hidden advantage in the looming confrontation with Congress: he got along well with the two of the leading Republicans on Capitol Hill. The new speaker, Joseph Martin of Massachusetts, was a newspaper publisher and a straight talker who loved the game of politics. In the Senate, the new chairman of the critical Foreign Affairs Committee was Michigan's Arthur Vandenberg, Senator Fulbright's would-be president. Despite his high-WASP name and elevated position on Capitol Hill, Vandenberg was a genial, popular legislator who shared Martin's background in journalism.

Truman celebrated the first day of 1947 by calling both Vandenberg and Martin to discuss the upcoming legislative session. Vandenberg told Truman that he ought to meet with the Senate's Republican leaders after his State of the Union speech on January 6. The president agreed. Martin told him that he was interested in cooperation, not confrontation, with the White House. "I am inclined to believe that he meant what he said," Truman wrote in his diary.[5]

He was in a chatty mood that day—chatty, and lonely. His wife and daughter were home in Independence. "Never so lonesome in my life," he wrote.[6] So the phone calls from the White House continued: to General Dwight Eisenhower, Navy Secretary James Forrestal, former Secretary of War Henry Stimson, former Labor Secretary Frances Perkins—and, of course, to Bess Truman. She and Margaret made plans to return to Washington in time for the president's State of the Union speech on January 6.

Under the Constitution, the president is obliged to deliver an annual report to Congress. It needn't be delivered verbally, and it wasn't for decades until Woodrow Wilson reestablished the tradition of speaking to a joint session of Congress, a tradition which fell into disuse after Thomas Jefferson's presidency. But while the annual exercise can be dull and pro forma, Truman's message in 1947 was freighted with political drama, for he would be speaking to a room filled with strangers—the new Republican congressmen and senators. Washington wondered if he would be conciliatory or confrontational, if he would adjust his ambitions to reflect November's elections or if he would continue to press ahead with his Fair Deal agenda.

The president spent the first few days of the new year polishing his address with Clark Clifford, the young Navy veteran who had become the man to see in the Truman White House. Clifford was one of several hidden hands that prodded Truman to take on John Lewis right after the election. When the confrontation worked out in Truman's favor, Clifford's star, already gleaming, gained even more luster.

The president, his family, and his top aides left the White House together on the morning of January 6 for the short ride to Capitol Hill. Bess and Margaret must have been exhausted, for their train from Missouri pulled into Washington's Union Station at seven that morning. The president walked from the White House to greet them.

The men in the president's party all wore fedoras as they posed for a team picture before the speech. Mrs. Truman looked like a woman who would have preferred to be somewhere else—perhaps in a comfortable bed after a long train ride. She wore a dark winter coat and a dark hat, declining the opportunity to smile for posterity's sake. But Margaret, in her fur coat and high heels, was beaming, as was her father.

Once inside the House chamber, the president gave his audience a chance to smile. As he began his speech, he looked out at the gathering and almost seemed to squint through his thick glasses. "It looks like a good many of you have moved over to the left since I was here last," he quipped. It took a moment for the joke to settle in, but once Truman's listeners realized he was kidding, they burst into laughter and a hearty round of applause, particularly from the left side of the chamber, where the Republicans sat in far greater numbers than months earlier.

The change in congressional leadership provided Truman with an opportunity to make a point as well as a quip. It framed the theme of his speech—the need to work together for the common good. Such sentiments weren't necessary when both Congress and the White House were in Democratic hands. But with government divided, Truman had little choice but to emphasize cooperation in pursuit of peace and prosperity. "I realize that on some matters the Congress and the president may have honest differences of opinion," he said, after first reminding his listeners that other presidents, including Woodrow Wilson and Herbert Hoover, faced a Congress run by the opposition. "On some domestic issues we may, and probably shall, disagree. That in itself is not to be feared. It is inherent in our form of government. But there are ways of disagreeing; men who differ can still work together sincerely for the common good." He made a point of reminding the nation that partisan differences did not interfere with wartime policy—Truman was very deliberately crafting a case for bipartisan agreement on foreign policy at a time of continued tensions with the Soviet Union.

Truman added to the theme of cooperation when he announced that he would continue to recommend the repeal of laws giving Washington broad powers over the economy. Ending these legacies of war, he said, would return decision making to "businessmen, farmers, and workers." Republicans were delighted to hear it, and they led the applause when Truman went on to promise to work for a balanced budget.

Truman struck a delicate balance as he addressed labor-management issues, one of the most contentious problems he had faced since the war's end. He urged that the new Congress, certain to be less friendly to labor than in the past, refrain from passing laws targeting the rights of labor. "We must not, under the stress of emotion, endanger our American freedoms by taking ill-considered action which will lead to results not anticipated or desired," he said. But he made it clear that he understood the public's anger with labor's militancy. He devoted more than five minutes of the forty-eight-minute speech to a four-point program designed to reduce strikes, particularly those called because of disputes between rival unions. He called for legislation against such strikes.

The end of extraordinary government power over labor and industry, while welcomed by the new Republican majority and others, posed a potentially grave problem in the postwar era. Government, he reminded his listeners, would soon no longer have the power to outlaw or take other action against the "paralyzing effects of a nationwide strike in such industries as transportation, coal, oil, steel, or communications," any one of which would lead to "a national disaster." He urged Congress to consider a mechanism to prevent an outbreak of strikes in vital industries.

He continued to find balance as he plowed through a laundry list of other domestic issues, from housing to aid for veterans to increased antitrust legislation. But while he calibrated his remarks to account for changed political circumstances, he did not abandon several key parts of the Fair Deal, including national health insurance. "I urge this Congress...

to provide adequate medical care to all who need it..." he said, adding that he hoped Congress would support establishment of a federal Department of Welfare.

With great subtlety, Truman followed a tribute to the nation's returned veterans with an appeal for new attention to civil rights. Thousands of African American veterans had returned home only to find segregation alive and well in the South and elsewhere. "Substantial segments of our people have been prevented from exercising fully their right to participate in the election of public officials," he said. "The will to fight these crimes should be in the hearts of every one of us." He told Congress that he had issued an executive order to establish a presidential commission on civil rights to study how Washington should enforce "federally secured civil rights." He moved from the subject without waiting for applause. None was forthcoming.

He closed this well-balanced, well-focused address on the nation's pressing issues with a flash of vision. Moving ahead, he said, the United States had an opportunity to "set the course of world history."

"If we maintain and strengthen our cherished ideals, and if we share the great bounty with war-stricken people over the world, then the faith of our citizens in freedom and democracy will be spread over the whole earth and free men everywhere will share our devotion to those ideas."

A day later, Truman appointed a new secretary of state, a man who would turn the closing sentiments of Truman's state of the union speech into reality. He was George C. Marshall.

Poverty in Greece led to concerns about a Communist takeover of the country. Here, aid workers distribute soup to poor Greeks.

CHAPTER 10

The Truman Doctrine

Speech to Joint Session of Congress
March 12, 1947

TRACK 10

T HE FIRST FULL YEAR OF PEACE MAY HAVE BEEN UNSETTLING IN THE UNITED States, leading to labor unrest and consumer discontent, but America's reconversion pains were nothing compared with the plight of Great Britain. Broke and overextended, the British Empire no longer ruled the waves, or very much else, as it had in the past. The government of Labor Party leader Clement Atlee, the British prime minister, believed it had to make a choice between overseas commitments and domestic tranquility at home. In early 1947, Atlee made his decision clear: Britain could no longer afford far-flung commitments of troops and money to help foil Communist insurgencies in southern Europe.

The Truman administration understood Britain's plight. The war left the British nearly bankrupt; their cities had been bombed during and after the Blitz; they lost another generation of men a mere twenty years after the slaughter of World War I; and the Atlee government had pledged to change the country's social and economic structures. An extremely cold and snowy winter made conditions even worse—factories and other workplaces were forced to shut down because of weather conditions, and coal was in short supply. Victory, for many ordinary Britons, had brought new hardships rather than great prizes and new riches.

Britain's domestic issues were a grave concern for America's foreign policy establishment because the British were very much a part of the U.S.-led effort to prevent the Soviets from expanding their influence in Europe. If the British were forced to reduce their commitments, the Soviets might be in position to take advantage of the power vacuum.

Those very fears were realized in late February 1947, when Atlee informed Truman that Britain could no longer afford to keep troops in Greece, where a strong Communist insurgency threatened the nation's pro-West government. The U.S. ambassador to Greece, Lincoln MacVeagh, told Washington that the situation there was "so critical that no time should be lost in applying any remedial measures." The government, he warned, could fall very quickly because of the public's lack of confidence and the growing strength of the insurgency. Britain had forty thousand troops in Greece to help defend the government's position, but in this critical moment, Atlee told Truman that he would withdraw all troops and economic aid from Greece by the end of March.

The impending British withdrawal, which was kept secret, had policy implications not only for Greece, but also for Turkey, which was battling an armed Communist movement as well. "If Greece was lost," Truman later wrote, "Turkey would become an untenable outpost in a sea of Communism."[1]

The president believed, as his new secretary of state put it, that the United States faced the first crisis in what could be a series of confrontations with the Soviet Union over Communist expansion beyond the Iron Curtain. Europe, the Middle East, and Asia all would be vulnerable to new Communist aggression if the United States did not respond to the threat in Greece, George Marshall said. During a flurry of meetings with his foreign policy team, Truman decided that Washington would come to the aid of both the Greeks and the Turks. "This was the time to align the United States of America clearly on the side, and the head, of the free world," Truman wrote.[2] Winning support for that position, however, would require national recognition that the days of U.S. isolationism truly were over, that the nation had new responsibilities in the world they could not evade. Truman was concerned that the new Republican-controlled Congress might rally again to the banner of isolationism rather than support a U.S. effort to assist the Greeks and Turks. "I knew that George Washington's spirit would be invoked against me, and Henry Clay's, and all the other patron saints of the isolationists," he wrote.[3] But the days of isolation belonged to another age. For Harry Truman, the crisis in Greece marked the moment when the United States finally put aside its traditional isolationism and assumed the mantle of world leader.

As Truman and his aides considered how to best apply American power in Greece and Turkey, they also began to craft a larger statement of U.S. policy toward the Soviet Union and Communist expansion. A book-length analysis of American policy toward the Soviet Union, written by Truman aides Clark Clifford and George Elsey, portrayed the Soviets as a growing impediment to world peace. They sought to retain a strong military presence in the nations of Eastern Europe, they were behind Communist political agitation in Western Europe, and they employed spies and other agents within the United States. The report urged that U.S. policy consider these larger issues rather than focus exclusively on whether the Soviets were complying with terms of postwar agreements. The United States ought to counter these aggressive Soviet moves, especially when democratic nations seemed at risk of falling into the Soviet orbit.

Truman considered the report to be so controversial that he asked that no additional copies be made, and that all copies—fewer than a dozen—already circulating be kept top secret. But he did not consider the report's conclusions to be unduly alarmist or unnecessarily negative. He too agreed that the time had come to challenge the Soviets. His new secretary of state, Marshall, was also more inclined than his predecessor, Byrnes, to confront Moscow. The president told the report's authors, Clifford and Elsey, to draft a major address not only about the situation in Greece and Turkey, but about the growing Soviet menace around the world.

The president chose to bring congressional leaders into the discussion, judging—correctly, as it turned out—that they would be more inclined to support Truman's position if they felt as though they were part of the discussions. A bipartisan group met with Truman, Marshall, and other foreign policy advisors on February 27, with Truman outlining Britain's still-unannounced plan to pull all troops and aid from Greece. The president told the legislators that he intended to help the Greeks and Turks resist Soviet expansionism, but he acknowledged that any such plan would require the cooperation and approval of Congress. Marshall, widely respected on Capitol Hill, told the delegation that the United States had two choices: act now, or lose.

Truman was heartened to find no opposition from several congress-men who, he wrote, had been "outspoken isolationists" in the past.[4] The gravity of the moment was not lost on anybody in the meeting. As Truman later said, the U.S. plan to aid Greece meant that the United States was "going into European politics."[5] It was one thing to fight Europe's wars. It was quite something else to become enmeshed in Old World politics, with all of its perceived cynicism and corruption. Truman and his aides argued that the United States no longer had a choice—according to the Clifford-Elsey report, Soviet influence had to be met with U.S. power, and now was the moment.

On March 7, Truman learned that his advisors believed that the Greek government was in imminent danger of collapse. The State Department supplied him with a draft of a speech he would give about Greece, but he rejected it. It read, he wrote, "like an investment prospectus."[6] He asked that the speech contain a sweeping statement of U.S. policy in relation to Communist expansionism. He didn't want words like "should." He wanted words like "must." The speech, he said, needed to be plain, direct, and clear, with no diplomatic code words meant to disguise intentions or encourage multiple meanings.

The president got what he asked for, although diplomats toned down some of Clark Clifford's robust anti-Soviet rhetoric. The final document was a straightforward, blunt assessment of the situation in Greece and Turkey, an argument in favor of American intervention there, and an unequivocal U.S. commitment to nations struggling to resist Soviet-inspired subversion. The broad promise to resist Communist expansion became known as the Truman Doctrine. "This," he later wrote, "was America's answer to the surge of expansion of Communist tyranny."[7]

He arrived on Capitol Hill at about one o'clock on the afternoon of March 12 and offered no forced smiles or waves to familiar faces. His tone was as somber as the dark suit he wore, and his audience immediately got the message. The senators and representatives gathered in the House chamber listened in silence as the president outlined a new venture in U.S. foreign policy. He opened with an explanation of the immediate crisis in Greece, telling lawmakers that the Greeks needed U.S. assistance "if Greece is to survive as a free nation." The Greeks were a poor, peace-loving country, victimized by the Germans during the war and now faced with "the terrorist activities of several thousand armed men, led by Communists…" The small Greek army needed help in order to resist the insurgency, he said.

He revealed that the British were no longer able to supply the Greeks with men and materiel because of their own domestic needs. Help, then, would have to come from the United States. Anticipating criticism that Greek democracy was flawed and undeserving of U.S. aid, Truman conceded that the government was "not perfect" and had "made mistakes." Immediately after the war, right-wing militia groups aligned with the government mounted a campaign against suspected Communist insurgents, leading to the murder of more than a thousand civilians.

"The extension of aid by this country does not mean that the United States condones everything that the Greek government has done or will do," he said. But Greek mistakes would not disqualify it from aid in the face of Soviet-inspired aggression.

Truman then made the case for aid to Turkey as well, arguing that while the situation was not as serious as in Greece, the Turks needed financial help to modernize and resist Soviet pressure. "We are the only country that can provide that help," he said.

The price for assisting the two countries was substantial: Truman asked Congress to approve $400 million in assistance over the following fifteen months. He also asked for authority to send U.S. armed forces to the two countries to train their security forces.

The power of this speech was not in its argument for aid to Greece and Turkey, urgent though it was. Rather, it became a foundational Cold War document because of the broader theme which Truman personally insisted upon. As he and his aides saw it, the struggle against Soviet Communism was not confined to the insurgency in Greece and Soviet pressure on Turkey. The threat was more global, and in many ways more insidious, than the armed conflict in Greece. Political movements in Western Europe took instruction and funding from Moscow, and sought to capitalize on postwar discontent in places like Italy and France. Communists were threatening the nationalist government of China, and were active in other corners of the world as well. The United States, Truman proclaimed, could not stand aside in the face of this threat.

"At the present moment in world history, nearly every nation must choose between alternative ways of life," he said. "The choice is too often not a free one. One way of life is based upon the will of the majority, and is distinguished by free institutions, representative government, free elections, guarantees of individual liberty, freedom of speech and religion, and freedom from political oppression." The second way of life, he argued, was based on "the will of a minority forcibly imposed upon the majority."

The United States *must*, he emphasized, "support free peoples who are resisting attempted subjugation by armed minorities or by outside pressures."

"I believe that we must assist free peoples to work out their own destinies in their own way," he continued, again emphasizing the word "must," written into the text at his insistence.

Nowhere in the speech was there a reference to the Soviet Union, but the target of his rhetoric was clear to the politicians gathered before him and his nationwide radio audience. "The free peoples of the world look to us in maintaining their freedoms," he said, building his case for the nation's inescapable role as a world leader. "If we falter in our leadership, we may endanger the peace of the world—and we shall surely endanger the welfare of this nation."

The implications of Truman's broad statement would influence U.S. policy for years to come. Nations large and small perceived to be under assault by Communism could expect American assistance. Many of those governments would prove to be as imperfect as Greece's, and some even more so. But the doctrine Harry Truman proclaimed on March 12, 1947, was never repudiated. It became, as he believed it must, American policy.

Three presidents—past, present, and future: Dwight Eisenhower and Herbert Hoover flank Truman at Princeton University.

CHAPTER 11

The Call of Public Service

Commencement Speech
at Princeton University
June 17, 1947

TRACK 11

F EW PEOPLE IMPRESSED HARRY TRUMAN MORE THAN HIS FORMIDABLE SECRETARY
of state, George C. Marshall. The general turned diplomat was,
in the president's eyes, the embodiment of genuine public service
and devotion to country. Quiet, modest, and seemingly without ego, the
sixty-six-year-old Marshall served at Franklin Roosevelt's side during
World War II as chief of staff of the nation's armed services. Marshall
retired after the war, and he and his wife began making plans for the next
stage of their lives. But those plans changed in an instant when President
Truman, concerned about the possibility of civil war in China between the
nationalist government and a Communist insurgency, called him at home
in mid-December. "General," Truman said, "I want you to go to China
for me."[1]

"Yes, Mr. President," he replied, asking no questions, declining to point
out that he had just retired, that his wife was concerned about his health and
was looking forward to a few restful years of peace and quiet. Marshall later
told Truman that he cut the conversation short because his wife was about
to enter the room, and he knew she would not be pleased to hear that he had
just agreed to travel halfway across the world on behalf of the United States.
Still, for Truman and for Marshall's many admirers, the former general's

unquestioning acceptance of the China mission spoke to his sense of duty and his selfless patriotism.

Marshall was popular with Republicans as well as Democrats, thanks in part to the respect he showed Congress during the war, when he kept Capitol Hill informed of strategy and other geopolitical issues. In early 1944, as the Allies were preparing to cross the English Channel to invade France, Marshall impressed Senator Harry Truman with his candor and confidence during briefings with the entire Congress. "There were many men in the Congress who harbored doubts and misgivings about the cross-Channel attack...but General Marshall came to Capitol Hill and spoke to about four hundred and fifty of us members of Congress, and his quiet, determined manner, his complete command of all the facts of the situation, quieted whatever fears anyone may have had," Truman recalled.[2]

Truman's appointment of Marshall as secretary of state belied the image of a White House staffed by provincial hacks chosen for their friendship rather than their talents. What's more, as secretary of state, Marshall presided over a department filled with brilliant, young deputies eager to play a role in shaping the postwar world. Diplomats who would become household names long after Truman left the White House—men like Dean Acheson, George Kennan, and Charles "Chip" Bohlen—were inspired by Marshall's leadership and by Truman's absolute confidence in him.

The postwar years were unlike any other time in U.S. history, and Truman and his advisors knew it. The United States was a superpower, sole possessor of a nuclear arsenal, richer than any of the war-torn countries of Europe, the world's arbiter, mediator, and enforcer. American diplomats were charged with resolving issues and problems certain to shape the world for decades to come. With the stakes so high, with the world so dependent on U.S. leadership, the importance of public service—the need for ambitious, visionary civil servants and government professionals—was critical if America wished to maintain its place as the world's most powerful nation.

Although critics often cited his connections to the Pendergast machine in Kansas City as a sign of his tolerance for crooked politics and cronyisms, Harry Truman was a man of ideals, few of which were stronger than his conception of public service. Later in life, Truman refused to serve on corporate boards or accept any position that, in his view, sought to capitalize on his presidency and his connections to top decision-makers in Washington.

He believed doing so would soil his years of service to his country. Well-versed in the history of ancient Rome, he found his ideal public servant in the story of Lucius Quinctius Cincinnatus, the Roman consul turned farmer who was summoned out of retirement to lead the republic in 458 B.C. After leading Rome's forces to victory over its enemies, Cincinnatus retired from power and returned to his farm. As Truman saw, Cincinnatus did his duty and asked for nothing in return. Duty was its own reward.

He found in Marshall a kindred spirit, and his admiration for his secretary of state knew no bounds. "The more I see and talk to him the more certain I am [that] he's the great one of the age," Truman wrote in 1947.[3]

If there were any questions about the competence of Truman's foreign-policy team, they were resolved in early 1947 under Marshall's leadership. Congress overwhelmingly approved Truman's request to aid Greece and Turkey, and the president's assertion that Washington would stand fast against the spread of Communism won him editorial support and public approval. Behind the scenes, Truman's foreign policy and military advisors began discussing the possibility of using aid to Greece and Turkey as a model for broader U.S. assistance for reconstruction in Europe. The discussion took on a sense of urgency when Marshall returned from a meeting of foreign ministers in Europe, convinced that the Soviets were intent on blocking reconstruction. By doing so, Marshall believed, they were hoping to fan the flames of discontent and perhaps even revolution in western and southern Europe.

Marshall, in a sense, saw Europe and Asia as Turkey and Greece writ large. If U.S. financial support could ward off Communism in those two countries, it followed that a broader commitment would do the same in other nations struggling in the aftermath of a catastrophic war. Truman, Marshall, and other advisors began to plot out a breathtaking program of financial assistance to all war-torn nations, including the Soviet Union. In Europe, American assistance would be used to encourage continental cooperation as a defense against Communism and as a means of dissipating the rivalries that plunged the world into war twice in a quarter-century.

Truman was scheduled to give a speech in Mississippi in early May to preview his cabinet's thoughts about American aid for reconstruction around the world. But Acheson, the under-secretary of state, delivered the speech in Truman's place when a scheduling conflict arose. Acheson's speech did not receive a great deal of attention, although it foreshadowed the reconstruction program that would become known as the Marshall Plan, named for the secretary of state. Acheson emphasized that the United States saw reconstruction of Europe as a continental issue, not as something to be carried out piecemeal, nation by nation. "The war will not be over until the people of the world can again feed and clothe themselves and face the future with some degree of confidence," he said.[4]

A month later, Marshall himself traveled to Cambridge, Massachusetts, to deliver the commencement address at Harvard University. The press did not receive a tip that Marshall's would be no ordinary commencement address, filled with bromides and advice to the new graduates. As a result, few reporters were on hand and even some of those did not fully appreciate what Marshall proposed: nothing short of massive American financial assistance to reconstruct the nations of Europe. It was a straightforward speech, befitting a man who told an aide who was compiling a report to "avoid trivia."[5]

Marshall's speech followed weeks of work behind the scenes as young go-getters at the State Department, most prominently George Kennan, devised a plan that deposited a mountain of earth on the grave of American isolationism.

It was logical for the United States to come to the aid of Europe, Marshall said in a crisp monotone. "Our policy is directed not against any country or doctrine but against hunger, poverty, desperation, and chaos." The careful wording had a plain purpose: American support for Europe's reconstruction was not meant as an act of aggression against the Soviet Union or against Communism. Of course, the plan indeed was designed to thwart the spread of Communism by easing the discontents that might encourage its growth. But Marshall's speech was temperate; his plan, inclusive. The Soviet Union was eligible for assistance, as were their vanquished enemies. But Marshall's message included a warning: "Any government which maneuvers to block the recovery of other countries cannot expect help from us."[6] Marshall surely had Moscow in mind as he read his lines.

The American offer to underwrite Europe's recovery created a sensation across the Atlantic. British and French foreign ministers organized a conference to develop a continent-wide response to the Truman administration's offer. Two countries behind the Iron Curtain, Poland and Czechoslovakia, were eager to participate, but, in a sign of Soviet opposition to the Marshall Plan, neither was permitted to attend. The Soviet foreign minister, Vyacheslav Molotov, denounced the plan as little more than an American plan to colonize Europe.

The Marshall Plan, formally known as the European Recovery Program, would win congressional approval and would go on to spend $13 billion to rebuild Europe. No Marshall Plan money was spent in Soviet-controlled Eastern Europe, where governments rejected the aid, or in Japan, where reconstruction was carried out under the direct control of General Douglas MacArthur. Historians today disagree over the long-term impact of the aid—some argue that Western Europe was already on its way to recovery and that the aid allowed France and the Netherlands to fight colonial wars, while others see the plan much as Molotov did, as a means to expand American business and power.

Whatever the plan's long-term effects, at the time of Marshall's speech and in the weeks following it, the shattered nations of Europe eagerly accepted Washington's offer of help. Truman saw the plan as "one of America's greatest contributions to world peace." Without it, he wrote, "it would have been difficult for Western Europe to remain free of the tyranny of Communism."[7]

Two weeks after Marshall's speech at Harvard, Truman traveled to another Ivy League campus, Princeton University in New Jersey, to deliver a commencement address and to accept an honorary degree. If the graduates and faculty were expecting the president to elaborate on his plans to rebuild Europe, they were disappointed. Truman was happy to have Marshall serve as the program's public face and chief advocate—it was, after all, his policy initiative in the first place. But such considerations have not always prevented presidents or other leading politicians from claiming credit for the ideas of their aides. Truman, however, was remarkably generous and secure as a chief executive, willing to share the public spotlight with a subordinate—or, at least, with a subordinate he respected and admired. While Truman certainly would have something to say about European reconstruction eventually, on this sunny spring day in Princeton, he preferred to talk about the need for public service in a world where the United States was a leader as never before.

Dressed in a natty double-breasted suit jacket, a handkerchief folded in his breast pocket, Truman addressed an audience that included the country's only living former president, Herbert Hoover, and his own eventual successor, Dwight Eisenhower, who took over as Army chief of staff after Marshall retired. Hoover's presence at the ceremony was a subtle reminder of American generosity after World War I, when millions of Europeans were dying of starvation and disease in the aftermath of that conflict's colossal destruction. Hoover organized an enormous relief effort to bring American food across the Atlantic, earning a reputation as one of the world's great humanitarians—a reputation he had lost while presiding over the first four years of the Great Depression. Hoover had been an outcast during Franklin Roosevelt's long presidency, but Truman invited him back to the White House to discuss how to feed those left hungry by yet another war. Hoover had not been back to the White House since he left office in 1933.

Truman opened his speech with an ad-libbed reference to a remark made by the university's president, Harold Willis Dodds, about the crises graduates would face. Directing his remark to Dodds, Truman said, "He should try sitting in my chair for about an hour and a half!"

Truman declared his thesis at the very beginning of his speech: the United States needed young, talented Americans to consider careers in public service. A new era had begun, an era during which the U.S. would "assume worldwide responsibilities and commitments." The nation's democratic ideals and its efforts to spread those ideals throughout the world would depend on "the quality of citizenship of our people."

For Harry Truman, citizenship meant more than casting a vote on Election Day, although that was important, and meant more than reading a newspaper or listening to radio newscasts. It meant more than engaging in a barstool debate, although any debate surely was better than none. It meant active engagement in service to the nation. "If our national policies are to succeed, they must be administered by officials with broad experience, mature outlook, and sound judgment. There is, however, a critical shortage of such men—men who possess the capacity to deal with great affairs of state."

Truman knew his critics saw him as a symbol of the very shortage he bemoaned. Just a few months earlier, even some Democrats publicly questioned his "capacity to deal with great affairs of state." But Truman had had a good spring, putting him in a comfortable position as he called on the nation's best and brightest to follow the example of people like George Marshall, although he didn't mention him by name. Equally unspoken was the reason behind his call to service. The government of the United States had grown fantastically during the New Deal and the war years. Now it was the most powerful state on earth. Maintaining and even expanding its new role would indeed require more administrators, more bright minds, than ever before. Universities, he said, ought to think of themselves as the training ground for a new corps of American public servants.

"In the task of finding and training men and women who will add strength to the public service," he said, "universities have a particular responsibility. They should develop in their students the capacity for seeing and meeting social problems as a whole and for relating special knowledge to broad issues. They should study the needs of government, and encourage men and women with exceptional interests and aptitudes along the necessary lines to enter the government service."

Truman himself was not a university graduate, nor were the men who mentored him in Kansas City—the Pendergasts and their retinue of aides. But the days of the old political machine were coming to an end. In their place, for better or worse, were government professionals—lawyers, advocates, social workers, middle managers who supervised bureaucracies created to deal efficiently and effectively with human problems. With this speech, Truman implicitly recognized that the world of politics and government had changed, or needed to change. The "difficult tasks of government today," he said, required the "systematic training of civilian employees once they have entered the public service." That training required a partnership between government and the nation's universities to ensure that those who "administer our far-flung enterprises" knew what they were doing.

Truman had something in mind besides encouraging universities to nurture careers in public service. Several days before his visit to Princeton, he was handed a 445-page report from a commission he appointed to study mandatory national service for all able-bodied males. The commission, which included Princeton's president, concluded that universal military service would spare the U.S. the expense of maintaining a huge standing army. Truman, who had been advocating mandatory training for all young males since the end of 1945, seized on the report's findings. He told his Princeton audience that universal national service was "the most democratic, the most economical, and the most effective method of maintaining the military strength we need."

Truman had told the commission's members that he did not consider universal training to be a strictly military measure. He believed the program would foster discipline, physical fitness, and civic responsibility. He elaborated on that theme in his Princeton speech. "The experience of living together and fulfilling a common responsibility should strengthen the spirit of democracy," he said. "It will be an experience in democratic living, out of which should come in increased measure the unity so beneficial to the welfare of the nation. We must remember, above all, that these men would not be training in order to win a war, but in order to prevent one."

The idea of national mandatory service found few advocates in Congress, to Truman's great frustration. His daughter and biographer, Margaret Truman, wrote that he regretted the proposal's failure for the rest of his life. Truman, his daughter wrote, was "convinced that if we had universal military training, there would have been no war in Korea, and possibly no war in Vietnam. The Communists would not have dared to challenge us because we would have been ready to respond with maximum strength and maximum speed."[8]

Coal yards became ghost towns as the nation's labor problems
led to a series of strikes and shutdowns in 1947.

Taking a Stand

Radio Address on the
Taft-Hartley Act
June 20, 1947

TRACK 12

THE NEW REPUBLICAN MAJORITY IN CONGRESS WAS EAGER TO TAKE ON THE nation's labor unions in 1947, after months of labor disruptions that tested the patience even of labor's friends and allies in Washington, Harry Truman included. There had been nearly five thousand strikes in 1946, involving 4.6 million workers in industries ranging from steel to meatpacking to coal. The Republicans interpreted their victory in November's congressional elections as a mandate to rein in the power of organized labor.

Slightly more than a third of the nation's work force was unionized in 1946. The nation's unions, so closely aligned with Franklin Roosevelt and the New Deal, saw their membership increase dramatically during World War II, going from about seven million in 1940 to more than fourteen million in 1945.

Republicans, the party generally aligned with capital and management, looked upon labor's growing power with dismay, none more so than Senator Robert A. Taft of Ohio. The son of William Howard Taft, who served as president from 1909 to 1913 and as chief justice of the Supreme Court from 1921 to 1930, Senator Taft was a leading spokesman for the midwestern wing of the party. Although often described as a strong congressional opponent of the New Deal, Taft was elected to the Senate in 1938, when most of the New Deal's reforms were already in place. Taft quickly developed a reputation as a probusiness, anti-union politician. He also emerged as one of Capitol Hill's strongest opponents of American assistance for Britain during the first two years of World War II. Before the Japanese attack on Pearl Harbor in December 1941, Taft argued vehemently against U.S. intervention, regarding it as Europe's problem, not America's.

Taft barely won reelection in 1944. Despite his close call, he risked further unpopularity in 1946 when he spoke out against the U.S.-led effort to prosecute Nazi war criminals in Nuremberg. During a speech that autumn, after the trials were over and a dozen prominent Nazis were condemned to death, Taft described the military tribunals as lawless and unfair. He argued that the prosecutions were not designed to achieve justice, but simply to exact revenge. And vengeance, he said, "is seldom justice."

Taft's views were wildly out of touch with the nation's sentiments. But even some Democrats grew to admire his willingness to risk his career over a matter of principle. It was hard to find anybody among the Allied powers who spoke up on behalf of justice for Nazis, but Taft did so. In 1956, three years after Taft's death, a young Senator from Massachusetts, John F. Kennedy, included Taft's stand against the Nuremberg trials in his Pulitzer Prize-winning book, *Profiles in Courage*.

Less celebrated, but almost as brave, was Taft's opposition to Truman's plan to draft striking workers during the bitter labor wars of 1946. The plan horrified union leaders and their allies in Congress, of course, but it also horrified Taft, who generally opposed anything labor wanted and supported measures the unions opposed. Taft's vigorous opposition made a deep impression on his colleagues in the Senate, even after the House overwhelmingly supported the president's plan. The Senate eventually rejected the measure, 70–13.

Taft was a Harvard Law graduate who was the antithesis of Harry Truman's bourbon-drinking, poker-playing friends. He was a poor retail politician who seemed uncomfortable with the back-slapping, hand-shaking rituals of campaign politics. But he was brilliant, principled, and ambitious, and was on his way to becoming the standard-bearer for Main Street Republicanism as it parted company with Eastern Establishment Republicans based in New York and Massachusetts.

The senator was not particularly fond of the president, whom he regarded as ill-suited for such a position of vast power. Truman respected Taft's integrity, but was appalled when the senator sought to block the nomination of David Lilienthal as head of the nation's Atomic Energy Commission in early 1947. Lilienthal was an original New Dealer who served as Franklin Roosevelt's head of the Tennessee Valley Authority, an agency many Republicans saw as quasi-socialist. Taft led opposition to Lilienthal's nomination to head the AEC, charging that he was "soft on the subject of Communism."[1] Such a person, Taft insisted, could not be trusted with the nation's atomic secrets. The Republican assault on Lilienthal, which included a more-than-faint whiff of anti-Semitism, failed when twenty of Taft's fellow Republicans broke ranks to support the nomination.

Nevertheless, Republicans had successfully raised the specter of Communists operating in the very heart of the federal government. As the Lilienthal matter neared its climax, Truman signed an executive order on March 21, 1947, requiring that federal employees take a loyalty oath and empowering the FBI to investigate the loyalty of workers. Truman's order, controversial to this day, had the political effect of countering the arguments of Republicans like Taft that Communists, or at least people who were insufficiently anti-Communist, were infiltrating the federal government while the president did nothing.

Having failed to bring down one target, Lilienthal, Taft turned to another—organized labor. Just as Lilienthal stood for something much larger than himself—he was one of the last New Dealers, and his defeat would have symbolized the new order of 1947—the nation's unions symbolized the left-of-center coalition that so successfully reduced Republicans to bystanders in the 1930s and early 1940s.

Republicans in the House of Representatives set the tone for a confrontation with labor in March 1947, when members passed a strong anti-union bill authored by Congressman Fred A. Hartley Jr. of New Jersey. Hartley was a Capitol Hill veteran, elected in the Herbert Hoover landslide in 1928. He managed to hold on to his seat in the face of massive Republican defeats through the Roosevelt landslides of the 1930s. Hartley despised labor's militancy, and within weeks of becoming chairman of the House Education and Labor Committee, he introduced legislation designed to revise the

New-Deal-era National Labor Relations Act, commonly known as the Wagner Act in honor of its sponsor, New York Senator Robert Wagner.

Under Hartley's proposal, unions would have been subjected to antitrust regulations and, in many cases, would have lost the right to bargain collectively with management. The bill also proposed a limit on labor's right to picket job sites. In a measure of Republican determination to reverse the New Deal, the House passed Hartley's bill with ease and passed it along to the Senate.

Robert Taft, as chairman of the Senate Labor and Public Welfare Committee, drafted his own bill, which was far less punitive than Hartley's legislation but which still sought to crack down on the power of unions. Taft's version of the bill did not include, for example, Hartley's ban on large-scale picketing, the abolition of the National Labor Relations Board, and measures designed to reduce organized labor's right to bargain collectively with management. The Senate passed Taft's bill, not Hartley's, so the two proposals were dispatched to a joint Senate-House conference committee. The result was a compromise, known as the Labor Management Relations Act of 1947, but more popularly remembered as the Taft-Hartley Act. The bill resembled the Senate version more than it did the House version. Under Taft-Hartley, limits were placed on labor's right to strike— strikes involving jurisdictional disputes between unions were banned, as were unauthorized, or wildcat, strikes and strikes called to express sympathy for another union's strike. Unions were banned from contributing to federal election campaigns, and union officials were forced to swear that they were not Communists. The closed shop, that is, a workplace allowed to hire only workers already in a union, was banned, and states were allowed to crack down on union demands to fire workers who refused to join a union. Unions were required to submit financial statements to members and to the U.S. Department of Labor. And the federal government was given increased power to intervene in labor-management disputes involving industries deemed vital to the national interest.

Taft-Hartley easily passed both houses in June and was sent to President Truman for his signature. Truman faced a genuine dilemma. He needed no lectures from the likes of Senator Taft about the inordinate power of labor and the maddeningly parochial concerns of some union leaders. By the same token, Truman had been a staunch supporter of labor while in the Senate and considered himself a friend of the average American worker.

Truman's cabinet was nearly unanimous in their support for Taft-Hartley, or, more properly, in their belief that the president ought to sign the bill and move on. The only exceptions were Labor Secretary Lewis Schwellenbach and Postmaster General Robert Hannegan, who, in his other role as chairman of the Democratic National Committee, was concerned about making an enemy of the nation's politically potent labor unions as the presidential election of 1948 drew closer. Truman believed that some form of curb on labor's right to strike was necessary, but overall, he believed the bill went too far in reversing the rights unions gained under the Wagner Act.

Still, he spent two weeks studying the bill and its implications for both management and union. His top political aide, Clark Clifford, joined the small chorus calling for a presidential veto. Truman relied on his young aide for sound political advice, and Clifford believed the time was right to take a stand—a stand which the nation's union members would notice and applaud.

Taft-Hartley set the stage for a memorable political duel between an embattled president and an aggressive Congress, with each side looking behind the legislation itself to its impact on the 1948 presidential election. Truman decided that Taft-Hartley was a bad piece of legislation and he also realized that a veto could be helpful in rallying union support in the '48 campaign. As his daughter, Margaret Truman, put it, Truman "was responding to his presidential conscience" but he also "did not by any means stop being a politician. The two are by no means incompatible."[2] But "incompatible" was a good word to describe the evolving relationship between leaders of the Republican Congress and the Democrat in the White House. "I've come to the conclusion that Taft is no good and Hartley is worse," Truman wrote. "Isn't it too bad that public men can't always be public servants?"[3]

The president vetoed Taft-Hartley on June 20, knowing full well that Congress had the votes to override his action. In the end, then, Taft-Hartley was destined to be a political defeat, but Truman was prepared to make Republicans work for their victory. At ten o'clock Eastern time on the night of June 20, hours after he sent Taft-Hartley back to Capitol Hill, Truman delivered a nationally broadcast address, explaining why he chose to veto the hotly debated issue. It took no small amount of courage to do so, for while Taft-Hartley was anathema to labor leaders, it had significant support among nonunion workers and, obviously, business leaders. And while union membership was strong, so too were memories of the long and bitter strikes of 1946.

Truman's veto certainly did help his standing among union workers, but there was no guarantee that his actions might not backfire with other Americans tired of strikes.

Truman opened his talk in his usual blunt fashion. He had vetoed the Taft-Hartley bill, he said, "because I am convinced it is a bad bill. It is bad for labor, bad for management, and bad for the country." His veto message, sent to Congress at noon that day, was long—more than five thousand words—and strong as he described Taft-Hartley as unworkable and unfair. In his radio address, Truman was even more emphatic. The bill, he said, was a "shocking piece of legislation."

"Under no circumstances could I have signed this bill. The restrictions that this bill places on our workers go far beyond what our people have been led to believe. This is no innocent bill…That is why I am speaking to you tonight. I want you to know the real meaning of this bill."

Republicans described Taft-Hartley as a moderate bill, which it surely was when compared with Congressman Hartley's original version. But Truman countered the Republican claim by insisting that there was more Hartley in the legislation than there was Taft.

"The bill is deliberately designed to weaken labor unions," he said. "It would take us back in the direction of the old evils of individual bargaining… If we weaken our system of collective bargaining, we weaken the position of every workingman in the country." With this language, Truman tied the fate of all workers to the bill, not just the 33 percent of workers who were union members. That was Truman's task: to persuade Americans that Taft-Hartley was not just an anti-union bill, but an antiworker bill.

Truman addressed the bill's main claim, that it would bring a measure of labor peace to the nation. "On the contrary," he said, "I am convinced that it would increase industrial strife." Labor, he said, would be forced to strike more often, not less, because of the bill's attack on union rights.

"One of the basic errors of this bill," he said, "is that it ignores the fact that over the years we have been making real progress in labor-management relations. We have been achieving slow but steady improvement in cooperation between employers and workers." Americans still had reason to fear labor disruptions, even if the sheer number of strikes was declining. Continued discontent in the nation's coal mines raised the possibility of another strike, possibly in the coming winter. The number of strikes was, in fact, down from the immediate postwar months, so Truman could argue that Taft-Hartley was more about the past than about the present.

Truman also framed the bill as the antithesis of America's vision of itself in the postwar years. "We seek in this country today a formula which will treat all men fairly and justly, and which will give our people security in the necessities of life. As our generous American spirit prompts us to aid the world to rebuild, we must, at the same time, construct a better America in which all can share equitably in the blessings of democracy."

Senator Taft responded to Truman's message with a radio address of his own, in which he defended the bill as a reasonable protection against the abuses of short-sighted unions. On June 24, Congress voted overwhelmingly to override Truman's veto, with many Democrats joining the Republican majority.

Ironically, in the years to come, Truman would use Taft-Hartley to intervene in several bitter labor disputes. He may not have liked the bill, but he was not averse to using the powers it gave him. To this day, Taft-Hartley remains on the nation's books despite several attempts to revise or abolish it.

Harry Truman addresses the NAACP on the Mall in Washington in an important moment in U.S. race relations.

CHAPTER 13

"I Mean All Americans"

Speech to the NAACP, Washington
June 29, 1947

TRACK 13

A S FRANKLIN ROOSEVELT'S SUCCESSOR, HARRY TRUMAN INHERITED THE remarkable political coalition FDR put together to implement his New Deal program during the Great Depression. For more than a dozen years, Roosevelt managed to persuade a disparate collection of voting blocs, regional interests, and racial and ethnic groups that they all had a common interest in the Democratic Party's agenda. Doing so required not only a bit of political magic, but also a willingness to make unpalatable compromises. Most of those compromises centered on race.

White Southern segregationists occupied powerful positions in the Democrat-controlled Congress of the New Deal years. Roosevelt needed their support to achieve his domestic reforms, and so was reluctant to challenge them, even when they deviated from the Democratic line to oppose some New Deal bills. At the same time, African Americans in the North were an important part of FDR's electoral coalition too, and Roosevelt's progressive rhetoric, along with the activism of his wife, Eleanor Roosevelt, raised expectations among African Americans. While Roosevelt did not champion specific civil rights legislation, the color-blind policies of New Deal agencies such as the Works Progress Administration and the Tennessee Valley

Authority offered work and opportunity to African Americans denied both, especially in the segregated South.

Roosevelt's popularity with African Americans worried Southern Democrats who presided over the region's repression of black citizens. FDR believed that he had to tread carefully on race, so he refused to support the efforts of Northern congressmen and senators from both parties to pass antilynching legislation. One such bill, cosponsored by Senator Robert Wagner of New York, a reliable New Dealer, would have punished local law enforcement officials if they failed to protect African American suspects from vigilante mobs. Southern sheriffs were often the key enforcers of the region's white supremacist order.

Racial tensions within the Democratic Party were put on hold, along with most other domestic concerns, during World War II. But when hundreds of thousands of African American veterans began returning home after fighting the racist regime of Nazi Germany, their expectations changed. They had served in segregated units in the armed services, were often assigned menial tasks (especially those who served aboard ships in the Navy), and now returned to a social order that consigned them to poorly served communities and denied them their basic civil rights. While all veterans were eligible for benefits from the GI Bill of Rights, and many African Americans took advantage of them, a black World War II veteran in the South could not attend public universities in the South, could be denied service at a lunch counter, and was expected to settle for separate but not equal public facilities, including water fountains, waiting rooms, and public transport.

As the postwar years unfolded, the race-based contradictions of the New Deal coalition could no longer be papered over in the name of a greater cause for, as time would show, it *was* the greater cause. Harry Truman's Democratic Party, home to civil rights advocates and staunch segregationists, the vehicle of black hopes and white defiance, was due for a prolonged conversation with itself.

Truman's life and career personified his party's contradictions and ambiguities on matters of race. He was a white man born in a border state, Missouri, a mere quarter century after the Civil War. His parents and neighbors had living memories of the war; his grandfather, Anderson Shipp Truman, owned several slaves. His everyday speech included racial epithets considered acceptable among white men of his generation. He was a creature of the U.S. Senate, a bastion of white male privilege and the home of some of the nation's most adamant segregationists. But Harry Truman also loved fair play and justice. While he was not without the prejudices of his generation, his region, and his race, he was devoted to the nation's founding ideals. State-sanctioned inequality offended his understanding of the American experiment in democratic rule. During his Senate reelection campaign in 1940, Truman told supporters at a political rally that he believed "in the brotherhood of man; not merely the brotherhood of white men, but the brotherhood of all men before the law." He noted that "Negroes have been preyed upon by all types of exploiters, from the installment salesman of clothing, pianos, and furniture to the vendors of vice. The majority of our Negro people find but cold comfort in shanties and tenements. Surely, as freemen, they are entitled to something better than this."[1]

While seemingly tepid when read in the twenty-first century, Truman's campaign speech displayed no small amount of courage for its time and place. It is noteworthy, too, because it was delivered during a difficult reelection campaign to an overwhelmingly white audience. Truman's statement of belief was not offered to would-be supporters from the African American community. He was talking to whites, many of whom would have found his sentiments offensive and dangerous. What's more, he did more than talk about the brotherhood of all men. He supported the antilynching legislation that Roosevelt opposed for political reasons.

In late 1946, Truman appointed a commission to study the state of civil rights in the United States. His action came in the wake of several violent racist outrages, including the murders of two black couples in Georgia. One of the men was a World War II veteran, and he was not the only black soldier to meet violence in the South not long after returning home from foreign battlefields. An African American sergeant was brutalized and left blind in Batesburg, South Carolina—the police and the town's mayor were implicated in the assault. In putting together the nation's first civil rights commission, Truman said he "wanted to get the facts behind these incidents...It was a simple approach to one of the oldest problems of a democratic society, yet the leaders of 'white supremacy' began at once their campaign of demagoguery" to halt development of "federal safeguards against racial discrimination."[2]

Before the commission's fifteen members (including Franklin D.

Roosevelt Jr.) began their work, Truman spoke to them in the White House in early January. His direction was clear—he said he wanted the nation's Bill of Rights implemented once and for all. After a century and a half, he said, it was time for the nation's basic set of rights to be applied to all its people, not just whites. Truman believed the government needed to be more aggressive, not only because it was right and fair, but also because he wanted to head off a revival of the Ku Klux Klan.

The commission spent ten months investigating the nation's broken promises to its black population, reporting back to the president in October 1947. The commission's report, entitled *To Secure These Rights*, documented in its 147 pages the ways in which African Americans were routinely deprived of their basic rights. The report inspired Truman to take a tougher stand for civil rights in 1948, leading to a bitter confrontation with his party's segregationists in an election year. "The main difficulty with the South is that they are living eighty years behind the times and the sooner they come out of it the better it will be for the country and themselves," Truman wrote.[3]

While the commission was in the middle of gathering its facts and organizing its recommendations, the National Association for the Advancement of Colored People invited Truman to speak at the closing session of its annual convention, to be held outdoors in front of the Lincoln Memorial on June 29, 1947. No president had ever addressed the NAACP since its founding in 1909, but Truman eagerly grasped the opportunity.

Ten thousand people gathered in front of the Mall's reflecting pool at the foot of the steps leading to the memorial. It was a pleasant June day. The president wore a light suit, with a white handkerchief tucked neatly in his breast pocket. Eleanor Roosevelt, wearing a black dress and hat, was among the honored guests seated at a podium on the memorial's staircase. An honor guard stood at attention behind Truman as he approached the podium at four thirty in the afternoon. A national radio audience listened in as Harry Truman—the grandson of a slave-owner, the son of a small town that celebrated the Confederacy's lost cause—delivered a speech whose sentiments, if not the words themselves, were worthy of the man whose image loomed over the proceedings, Abraham Lincoln.

Truman, or more precisely, Truman's speechwriters, did not have Lincoln's poetic sense of language. But the speech's plain, direct approach to the nation's oldest and most intractable problem left no doubt where

Truman stood on the issue on the eve of what promised to be a contentious election campaign. "I should like to talk to you briefly about civil rights and human freedom," he began, looking out on the thousands standing at the foot of the great memorial's staircase.

"It is my deep conviction that we have reached a turning point in the long history of our country's efforts to guarantee freedom and equality for all our citizens. Recent events in the United States and abroad have made us realize that it is more important today than ever before to insure that all Americans enjoy these rights. When I say all Americans, I mean all Americans."

It was a theme—"all Americans"—he returned to repeatedly during his speech. By doing so, he was reminding his white listeners on radio that the rights they enjoyed should not be theirs alone. Such an assertion cut to the core of white supremacist ideology. Segregationists and their sympathizers, after all, believed that the rights of citizenship did not belong to "all Americans."

Truman did not explain why he believed the nation was at a turning point, but perhaps it wasn't necessary. His presence at an NAACP convention was a milestone in the organization's history, and in the broader history of race relations. The political power of white supremacist Democrats was not broken, but Truman's speech indicated history was moving in a new direction.

"Our immediate task is to remove the last remnants of the barriers which stand between millions of our citizens and their birthright," he said, speaking more to his fellow leaders than he was to his audience. "There is no justifiable reason for discrimination because of ancestry, or religion, or race, or color...Every man should have the right to a decent home, the right to an education, the right to adequate medical care, the right to a worthwhile job, the right to an equal share in making the public decisions through the ballot, and the right to a fair trial in a fair court.

"To these principles I pledge my full and continued support."

Some of Truman's aides and fellow Democrats, while sympathetic to civil rights in the abstract, were concerned about roiling the party's brittle coalition as the election year of 1948 approached. Several advised him to move slowly on civil rights to avoid alienating a region he would need to win a second term. Truman explicitly addressed that advice in his speech to the NAACP. Noting that many "of our people" suffered insult, intimidation, intolerance, and physical assault, the president said postponing a confrontation with oppression was morally impossible.

"We cannot wait another decade or another generation to remedy these evils," he said. "We must work, as never before, to cure them now."

The urgency was based on simple moral outrage: discrimination and racial violence were crimes against the nation's highest ideals. But there was another reason why Truman wished for an immediate cure. As the hard peace of a Cold War descended on the world, the United States was engaged in a protracted war of ideas with the Soviet Union. Truman suggested that denying equal rights to racial minorities weakened America's case against Communist propaganda. "Our case for democracy," he said, "should be as strong as we can make it." Otherwise, nations "beset by every kind of privation" might reject democracy as imperfect and instead "surrender to the false security" of totalitarian rule.

After pledging to provide the federal government with better tools to enforce fairness and equality, and after paying tribute to Mrs. Roosevelt's presence on the podium, Truman closed with a quote from Lincoln, whose words were carved into the marble walls behind him. "We shall remain a united people," Lincoln said during another struggle nearly a century earlier.

Truman's wish for unity would not be realized, but within a year of this speech, he signed executive orders desegregating the federal work force and the nation's armed services.

With Republican leaders Joseph Cannon and Arthur Vandenberg
behind him, President Truman challenges his political opponents
to act on their proposals as the elections of 1948 beckoned.

CHAPTER 14

Challenging the "Do-Nothing" Congress

Address Opening a Special Session of Congress

November 17, 1947

TRACK 14

D EMOCRATS, TO THEIR SURPRISE AND DELIGHT, HAD REASON TO LOOK FORWARD to the coming presidential campaign of 1948. The Republican-controlled Congress did not steamroll Harry Truman—rumors of the president's irrelevancy clearly were exaggerated. A Gallup poll taken in July of 1947 showed that 55 percent of those polled believed they would support a Democrat the following year. That represented an increase of nearly ten points in just seven months. George Gallup, the poll's founder, said that the Democrats had managed to pull off "a major political feat."[1] What's more, the president's approval rating reached 60 percent in a Gallup poll in late spring.

While the public opinion pendulum would swing back against Truman toward the end of 1947, it seemed that some Americans were reconsidering their opinion of feisty Harry Truman. Liberals, itching to make a stand against those who wished to roll back the New Deal, loved his veto of Taft-Hartley. African American voters, who were becoming an important voting bloc in Northern cities, appreciated his aggressive stand on civil rights. The change in public sentiment heartened Truman's advisors, especially young Clark Clifford, the strategist who had urged the president to veto Taft-Hartley and to confront the nation's racial problems.

Clifford began preparing for the '48 campaign during the summer of 1947. With Truman's approval, Clifford reached out to Democrats to identify ideas and themes for the president's election bid. One major concern was the very public presence and unknown intentions of Henry Wallace, FDR's former secretary of agriculture and vice president—the man who was tossed off the national ticket in favor of Truman at the 1944 Democratic convention. Since Truman fired him as secretary of commerce in late 1946, Wallace had become a popular figure among the party's most liberal activists, and he was not shy about criticizing his former boss, Harry Truman. The implicit message was clear: Truman was no Franklin Roosevelt. Wallace's audiences were free to conclude that they needed a new face to revive the fallen president's legacy.

Most mainstream Democrats, especially the party's urban bosses, had little respect for Wallace as a political operator, so they were not particularly worried about a possible primary challenge to Truman. More worrisome, however, was the potential of a Wallace third-party candidacy. He couldn't win on a third party line, but he surely could steal enough Democratic votes to hand the election to the Republicans. Democrats knew what happened in 1912, when former President Theodore Roosevelt, a Republican, ran as a third-party candidate against incumbent President William Howard Taft, also a Republican, and Democrat Woodrow Wilson. The Republican vote was split between the two presidents, allowing Wilson to squeak in with less than 50 percent of the vote. That scenario haunted Democratic strategists in 1947.

A more significant question centered on the president's intentions. Would he run for a full term in his own right? In those days before marathon primary seasons and two-year presidential campaigns, candidates did not feel the need to announce their intentions until the election year was underway. Truman went along with Clifford's effort to put together a campaign strategy, but his precise intentions remained unclear. He occasionally talked about the presidential prospects of Dwight Eisenhower, the supreme commander of Allied forces in Europe during World War II. Truman thought many Democrats might turn to the popular Eisenhower as an alternative to him in 1948, a prospect he sometimes seemed to embrace. He knew his wife, Bess, disliked Washington and the White House, and he had his own misgivings about the presidency. "Aside from the administrative burden," he wrote, a president "has to take all sorts of abuse from liars and dema-gogues...The people can never understand why the president does not use his supposedly great power to make 'em behave. Well, all the president is, is a glorified public relations man who spends his time flattering, kissing, and kicking people to get them to do what they are supposed to do anyway."[2] No person, he insisted, would wish to be president "if he knew what it entails."[3]

If Truman seemed something less than his usual ebullient self in the summer of 1947, it had more to do with personal grief than despair over his job and prospects. His beloved mother, Martha, died on the morning of July 26 at the age of ninety-four. Truman was devoted to her, and, just weeks earlier, he had spent twelve days with her in Missouri after she broke her hip. When he heard that she might be near death—not the first time such a report reached the White House—Truman prepared to fly immediately to Missouri. But she died before he could reach her bedside.

The president's mother was born in an age and a state that permit-ted human beings to own other human beings. She made no secret of her admiration for Confederate heroes like Robert E. Lee and others. And she had lived to see her son, the president of the United States, demand that the grandchildren of slaves be accorded the rights of citizenship promised in the aftermath of the Civil War.

Truman buried his mother on July 28, remembering her reaction to news that her son would become the nation's chief executive. "When I succeeded Franklin Roosevelt," Truman wrote, "my mother had so wisely said it was no occasion for her to rejoice. She said that she could only feel grieved that President Roosevelt had died."[4]

Now the question was whether Martha Truman's son would run for a term as president in his own right, without the shadow of Franklin Roosevelt hovering over him.

He decided he would, although he did not announce his candidacy until early February 1948. In later years, Truman explained that he chose to run because he believed "that this was no time for a new and inexperienced hand to take over the government and risk the interruption of our domestic pro-gram and put a dangerous strain on our delicately balanced foreign policy."[5] That was quite a claim, considering how unprepared Truman himself was when he was thrust into the presidency in April 1945, with a global war to manage. But Truman also saw himself as a defender of Roosevelt-style liberalism as it came under attack from the Republican leaders of the 80th Congress. The prospect of campaigning against foes he regarded as backward and reactionary had more than a little appeal.

In November, Clifford reported back to Truman after weeks of reflecting on the coming campaign and meeting with fellow Democrats. He delivered a long report to the president that predicted, correctly, that New York Governor Thomas E. Dewey would win the Republican nomination, as he did in 1944, and that Henry Wallace would run as a third-party candidate to Truman's left. Less shrewdly, Clifford believed that the South would support Truman because it was so reliably Democratic. In fact, Clifford said, the South was so solidly Democratic that it could be ignored while the president focused on other key constituencies, such as Catholics, who were worried about Communism, African Americans, who wished to hear more about Truman's civil rights positions, and labor leaders, who cheered Truman's veto of Taft-Hartley but resented the president's criticisms of strikes and other labor agitation.

The South, in fact, would revolt against Truman, but that disastrous scenario would not unfold for several months.

Clifford's memo foresaw problems on Truman's left. With Wallace looming as a possible drain on liberal voters, Truman had to demonstrate his progressive bona fides to win over possible defectors and transform Wallace from a threat to a mere curiosity. Republicans in Congress would serve as a useful target for the president as he prepared for the campaign trail.

On November 17, 1947, around the time he received the Clifford memo, President Truman addressed members of Congress called to Capitol Hill for a special session. The session and the speech itself are noteworthy not so much for what they accomplished, or didn't, but because of the precedent Truman established. In hauling Congress to Capitol Hill in November 1947, Truman displayed his eagerness to challenge Republican leaders for control of Washington's agenda. He would do so again, with even more drama, in July 1948, in the middle of his extraordinary election campaign.

On this occasion, Truman stepped to a podium in the House chamber to tell Congress that the demands of the world and of the domestic economy required their unscheduled appearance on Capitol Hill. Behind the president sat the Republican leaders of Congress: Senator Arthur Vandenberg, wearing a dark bow tie, and Speaker Joseph Martin, his hair unnaturally dark, his face gaunt and serious. All three men were born in 1884. Children of the nineteenth century, they sought to lead the United States into a new and unknowable era of world leadership in the middle of the twentieth century. While Truman saw himself as the embattled defender of liberalism in the face of Republican reaction, the men behind him on this occasion were hardly enemies. Truman liked and admired both of them in the clubby, collegial way of Capitol Hill, circa mid-century.

Truman told Congress that nothing less than the "future of the free nations of Europe" and the "future of our own economy" were at stake in the autumn of 1947. Three European nations, Austria, France, and Italy, needed hundreds of millions of dollars to get through the winter without starvation and deprivation. Meanwhile, inflation threatened to bring the promise of postwar prosperity to a bitter end.

The massive spending program known as the Marshall Plan had yet to win acceptance in Congress. In the meantime, Truman said, Europe needed massive emergency assistance. Without it, Truman said, the world could return to war once again. "Our people know that our influence in the world gives us an opportunity—unmatched in history—to conduct ourselves in such a manner that men and women of all the world can move out of the shadows of fear and war and into the light of freedom and peace…Human misery and chaos lead to strife and conquest. Hunger and poverty tempt the strong to prey upon the weak."

Although Senator Vandenberg was an internationalist, Truman was convinced that many of Vandenberg's colleagues remained skeptical of America's role in restoring Europe to peace and prosperity. "In foreign affairs," he later wrote, "the Republican leadership was still suffering the aftereffects of isolationism." A "selfish Republican majority" might easily block initiatives like the Marshall Plan, he believed.[6] He intended to work with Vandenberg and other like-minded Republicans to twist arms on behalf of starving, war-torn Europe.

At home, the threat was not starvation but high prices. "Since the middle of 1946," he noted, "wholesale textile prices have gone up by 32 percent [and] building materials have gone up 42 percent. Wholesale prices on the average have gone up 40 percent." He asked Congress to consider the plight of the "housewife who goes to buy food today." She would have to spend $10 for groceries that cost her $7 a year and a half earlier.

Fueling inflation was an explosion of credit, a development that Truman, a very traditional man who didn't even own his own home, found troubling. "At a time when the economy is already producing at capacity," he said, "a further expansion of credit simply gives people more dollars to use in bidding up the prices of goods." The Federal Reserve, he said, ought to step in to tighten credit, but it lacked the legislative authority to do so.

Truman sought greater authority over the private economy, a request he knew most Republicans would find appalling. Some private, unregulated transactions were a threat to the nation's stability, he said. "Grain, for example, is too badly needed to permit wasteful feeding to livestock," he said. "Steel, as another example, is too scarce to be used for nonessential purposes." He asked Congress for legislation giving the federal government power to allocate "scarce commodities" rather than rely on unregulated market forces. He also asked for more power to regulate the nation's exports. "Goods that we cannot wisely export must be kept here, and the shipments we make must go where they are needed most." The president also asked for power to tighten the nation's rent-control laws, which allowed increases of up to 12 percent a year.

Truman's speech was a bold argument in favor of continued federal power over the marketplace, one doomed to die a slow death in a Republican-ruled Congress. But it put Congress on the defensive, and set in motion events that would lead to his memorable campaign against a body he would soon call the "do-nothing 80th Congress."

In the early hours of July 15, 1948, Harry Truman tried to rally his divided party at the Democratic National Convention.

CHAPTER 15

Abandoned

Acceptance Speech at the Democratic National Convention in Philadelphia
July 15, 1948

TRACK 15

ALTHOUGH HE ENJOYED A BLIP OF NEWFOUND POPULARITY IN 1947, THE PRESI-dent's approval ratings began to sink again as Republican contenders battled each other for the right to challenge Truman—assuming that he was indeed the Democratic Party's nominee. Some Democrats held out hope that Dwight Eisenhower might make himself available as a possible replacement for Truman at the top of the ticket. Nobody was quite sure of Eisenhower's politics or even his political affiliation, but he was popular and he could be a winner in November.

An article in *Time* magazine, a reliable barometer of conventional political wisdom, hailed the idea of Truman giving way to Eisenhower, while *The Nation* magazine, a liberal journal, reported that some Democrats desperately wished that Truman would take himself out of the running. Democrats felt that the president was "not equipped to deal with the monumental problems of the times," the magazine reported.[1] A Gallup poll taken in March showed that Truman was trailing all of the prospective Republican challengers—New York governor Thomas Dewey, who lost to FDR in 1944, former Minnesota governor Harold Stassen, Truman's friend in the U.S. Senate, Arthur Vandenberg of Michigan, and the commander of U.S. ground forces in the Pacific during World War II, General Douglas

MacArthur. Another Gallup poll taken in mid-April found that only 36 percent of respondents approved of Truman's performance, down from 55 percent in the fall of 1947.

His fellow Democrats were distraught, but Truman seemed surprisingly sanguine. "I never paid any attention to the polls myself," he later wrote, "because in my judgment they did not represent a true cross-section of American opinion."[2] That said, however, Truman was well aware that his party and supporters were concerned, and those concerns could become self-fulfilling. The press fueled Democratic anxieties, leading voters to conclude that Truman was a lost cause. Truman was concerned not so much about the poll's findings but their impact on opinion leaders and voters. Even "the most intelligent and well-meaning people," he wrote, might write off his chances not on the merits, but on false perceptions.

While politicians and the press dissected Truman's chances of reelection, the president himself was confronted with problems of a very different sort. In February, Truman asked Congress to pass a civil rights law that would, at last, make lynching a federal crime and that would better protect African Americans against measures designed to suppress their vote, such as the poll tax. Southern Democrats were outraged, and more than fifty Southern Democrats announced that they would vote against any such measures designed to destabilize white supremacy in the region. Alabama's two senators, Lister Hill and John Sparkman, visited Truman in the White House to tell him that they would not support his renomination. The prospect of a split in the party made the already dismal polls seem more like a harbinger of defeat. It was inconceivable that Harry Truman could win reelection without the Solid South.

On the international stage, the Truman administration was grappling with high politics in the Middle East. Zionist organizations were demanding a Jewish homeland in British-ruled Palestine, and some were already fighting to achieve that long-sought goal. A Zionist group called Irgun fought Arabs and British alike in an attempt to establish Jewish control over a portion of Palestine, while Arabs in the region led raids on Jewish homes and settlements. The British had ruled Palestine since the end of World War I, but London's new postwar government announced that it would withdraw its troops and administrators from the area in mid-May. Palestine would become a problem for the United Nations to resolve.

Harry Truman met with many advocates who supported the foundation of a Jewish state, but none was as effective as Truman's longtime friend and former business partner, Eddie Jacobson, who pleaded with Truman to meet with Chaim Weizmann, the aging leader of the global Zionist movement. Grudgingly, Truman agreed to the meeting, although Weizmann was whisked into the White House with no public notice on March 18—even the State Department didn't know about the meeting. Despite confusion, mixed signals, and dissent within his administration, Harry Truman immediately recognized the new state of Israel, eleven minutes after it was proclaimed on May 14, 1948. "I was told that to some of the career men of the State Department this announcement came as a surprise," Truman wrote. "It should not have been if these men had faithfully supported my policy."[3]

Early summer would bring a new crisis in another partitioned land, this one in Germany. In an attempt to force the United States, Britain, and France out of West Berlin, the Soviet Union refused to allow ground deliveries of food and other supplies to the western portion of the city. Truman ordered West Berlin to be resupplied from the air, with dozens of cargo planes dropping thousands of pounds of food and other necessities by parachute. The Berlin Airlift would go on to become an extraordinary public relations victory for the United States and a major success for the president.

While Truman's support for Israel won him the gratitude of many American Jews, the president's political fortunes continued to decline as the two parties prepared for their national conventions. In early June, Truman set out on a cross-country train tour covering thousands of miles and nearly twenty states. The trip was billed as "nonpolitical," but that was a polite fiction. The president made sure to attend to some ceremonial business during the journey, but there was little question about the real purpose of the exhausting agenda. "On this nonpartisan, bipartisan trip that we are taking here," Truman said at one point, "I understand that there are a whole lot of Democrats present too."[4]

Truman found himself delivering feisty, spontaneous speeches from the back of the sixteen-car train, a formula he would revisit with great success later in the year. Listeners seemed to enjoy the president's informality and off-the-cuff speeches—in Los Angeles, a million people cheered and waved as Truman and his party traveled by car through the city's streets—but the unscripted performances often did nothing to counter poor public perceptions of the administration. During a speech in Oregon, a tired Truman told an audience that he liked "Uncle Joe" Stalin, describing him as a "decent fellow," a remark that created controversy at the time and one that would haunt the president during the rise of Senator Joe McCarthy in the early 1950s.[5] Still, the long train ride prepared Truman for the campaign to come, but did little to produce a change in public opinion.

The Republican Party convened in Philadelphia in mid-June and, for the second time, they nominated Thomas Dewey of New York as their presidential candidate. Dewey did well as a sacrificial lamb in 1944, when nobody expected Franklin Roosevelt to lose his bid for a fourth term. Now, with Roosevelt dead and his successor stumbling badly, Dewey was treated as a president-in-waiting. Republican Congresswoman Clare Boothe Luce summed up conventional wisdom when she described Truman as a "gone goose," to the wild applause of cheering Republican delegates.[6]

Over the July 4 weekend, James Roosevelt, son of the late president, contacted more than a dozen top Democrats, urging them to join him at an emergency meeting before the party's convention to discuss a plan to replace Truman with Dwight Eisenhower on the convention floor. Roosevelt's contact list offered a glimpse of the widespread dissatisfaction with Truman. Among those expressing interest in the Eisenhower bid were Mayor Frank Hague of Jersey City, perhaps the ultimate urban boss, Mayor Hubert Humphrey of Minneapolis, an earnest young liberal, and Governor Strom Thurmond of South Carolina, a staunch segregationist. Labor leaders and other Democrats joined the growing pro-Eisenhower movement, but the retired general, now serving as president of Columbia University in New York, announced on July 9 that he would not be a candidate under any circumstances.

Demoralized and dispirited, the Democrats descended on Philadelphia—the very city where Republicans had nominated Dewey three weeks earlier—on July 12. The mood in the city's hotel lobbies, bars, and restaurants was a good deal more subdued that it was during the Republicans' boisterous convention. Many Democrats agreed with Congresswoman Luce's assessment of their president. A wire service report on the eve of the convention noted that Democrats "act as though they have accepted an invitation to a funeral."[7] The convention's keynote speaker, Alben Barkley of Kentucky, got the crowd going with a rousing, hour-long speech on opening night, impressing Truman and leading to his nomination as Truman's vice-presidential candidate. But the next day's session offered a glimpse of the disaster that awaited Truman and his party. Liberals demanded a strong civil rights plank in the party platform, a plank that would, in essence, reiterate much of what Truman had already said, pledged, or actually achieved. Mayor Humphrey, one of the leaders of the civil rights faction, delivered an impassioned speech challenging delegates to support a strong statement of support for the nation's black population. He explicitly criticized Southern support for state's rights, saying it was time the United States acted on human rights. Humphrey's speech carried the day. The civil rights plank passed, to the chagrin and disgust of the party's powerful Southerners. One of Truman's key advisors, a New York political operative named Edward J. Flynn, privately told Humphrey that the stronger civil rights plank was precisely what the party needed, but others in the White House, including the president, were extremely worried that the South might bolt the party.

The fight over civil rights continued the following evening, July 14, although the main event was supposed to be Truman's formal nomination as the party's candidate and his acceptance speech. A delegate from Alabama delivered a caustic speech about the party's civil rights plank and promptly left the convention hall in a huff, along with a dozen other delegates from Alabama and all twenty-three from Mississippi. The remaining Southern Democrats remained in their seats, sullen but present as the balloting began for president. By the time all the nominating and seconding speeches were done and the count finished, it was after midnight. Truman sat through the deliberations in a private office, waiting to deliver his acceptance speech to delegates and a national radio audience. He didn't get the chance until about two o'clock in the morning.

As a band played "Hail to the Chief" and exhausted delegates tried to summon some enthusiasm for their standard-bearer, the president of the United States strode confidently to a podium bristling with radio microphones. Truman was dressed in a white summer suit, and he seemed no worse for the wear after sitting through hours of speeches in the stifling heat of a convention hall without air-conditioning.

As disoriented pigeons circled wildly—a gimmick gone wrong as part of the convention fanfare—Harry Truman began the most important speech of his life with an energy and enthusiasm that seemed to take his listeners by surprise. After apologizing for the microphones that prevented some delegates from seeing his face and after thanking the convention for nominating Barkley as his vice president, Truman got right to his point in his clipped, midwestern cadence: "Senator Barkley and I will win this election and make these Republicans like it—don't you forget that! We will do that because they are wrong and we are right, and I will prove it to you in just a few minutes."

Any delegate or radio listener who expected to hear the mournful tones of a man heading to certain defeat must have been shocked to hear this feisty, confident candidate who apparently hadn't been told that he was doomed. Truman's cross-country tour in June had given him an opportunity to test out some campaign themes and rehearse the combative style that would become his trademark in the summer of 1948.

Truman's opponent, Dewey, had already established himself as an aloof, above-the-battle figure who spoke in confident platitudes. The president, in this speech, cast himself as an anti-Dewey: he was specific, he was passionate, and he was aggressive. And he was not above playing the Hoover-Depression card as he warned his radio audience of the last time Republicans held the White House.

Democrats would win in November, he said, because "the Democratic Party is the people's party, and the Republican Party is the party of special interest, and it always has been and always will be." Delegates, hearing this summons to battle, cheered wildly, hoping that they were witnessing a turning point in the campaign.

He challenged traditional Democratic voters who were thinking about Dewey and the Republicans. Farmers, for example, never had it so good— and Truman said so. "Never...were the farmers of any republic or any kingdom or any other country as prosperous as the farmers of the United States," he said, "and if they don't do their duty by the Democratic Party, they are the most ungrateful people in the world!" Truman had similar words for the labor movement, noting that wages and salaries increased from $29 billion per year in 1933 to more than $128 billion in 1947. "And I say to labor what I have said to the farmers: They are the most ungrateful people in the world if they pass the Democratic Party by this year." More cheers from the delegates, more thoughts that perhaps they hadn't made a mistake after all. Maybe Harry Truman was made of sterner stuff.

Having reminded his fellow Democrats of their duty, Truman turned his attention to the Republican-controlled 80th Congress. He turned back the clock to 1932, blaming Republicans for the country's dire plight that year and tying the Republicans of 1948 to the Republicans of that earlier era. He accused them of standing by while he sought to control prices, improve housing, create better labor relations, increase the minimum wage, and increase the pay of teachers. "I wonder if they think they can fool the people of the United States with such poppycock as that," he said.

It was not the sharpness of Truman's attacks that caught his listeners' attention. After all, his predecessor, Franklin Roosevelt, was no slouch when it came to campaign-style assaults on the opposition. And the Republicans had spared little in their gleeful condemnations of Truman's tenure during their convention in Philadelphia weeks earlier. But Truman's folksy, informal delivery—his use of the word "poppycock"—certainly registered with delegates and the radio audience. Americans were not used to hearing their presidents use that kind of informal language to describe the plans of their opponents. Truman lacked Roosevelt's debonair delivery, but what he lacked in polish, he made up in passion.

He didn't shy away from the issue that infuriated his Southern colleagues, but he tried to use it to draw a distinction between his party and his opponents. "Everybody knows that I recommended to the Congress the civil rights program," he said, gesturing with both hands. "I did that because I believe it to be my duty under the Constitution. Some of the members of my own party disagree with me violently on this matter. But they stand up and do it openly! People can tell where they stand. But the Republicans all professed to be for these measures. But Congress failed to act."

He found his theme—Congress, in the hands of Republicans for the first time since the Hoover Administration, had stood idly by while he grappled with the nation's difficult issues. His critics talked of the measures they supported, but they refused to use their power to pass the required legislation. So, in a surprise move that delighted the delegates, he issued a challenge. He noted that the Republican platform consisted of a laundry list of promises—to bring down high prices, for example, and to ease the nation's housing problems. Truman said he agreed that these were issues requiring urgent attention. "My duty as President requires that I use every means within my power to get the laws the people need on matters of such importance and urgency," he said. "I am therefore calling this Congress back into session on July 26." Delegates were stunned. Calling Congress back into session in midsummer was not for the faint of heart. Truman tried this gambit in late 1947, but that special session took place in November, in a year without important elections. This time, Truman was calling Congress back in midsummer of an election year. He would not be making many friends from either party.

Truman noted that the special session would begin on a day, July 26, "which out in Missouri we call 'Turnip Day.'" The session that followed became known as the "Turnip Session."

"Now, my friends, if there is any reality behind that Republican platform, we ought to get some action from a short session of the 80th Congress," he said. "They can do this job in fifteen days, if they want to do it. They will still have time to go out and run for office.

"They are going to try to dodge their responsibility. They are going to drag all the red herrings they can across this campaign, but I am here to say that Senator Barkley and I are not going to let them get away with it."

Truman's performance during the wee hours—it was nearly three o'clock in the morning by the time he finished—was one of his best. He gave the exhausted delegates something to cheer about, something to give them hope for the long campaign to follow.

Truman, satisfied, outlined his strategy in his diary. "I'm going to attempt to make them meet their campaign promises before the election," he wrote.[8] He had no doubt how that would turn out.

But even as grumbling congressmen and senators returned to Washington's midsummer heat, two events took the air out of Truman's campaign and, in the minds of many, all but finished him. Two days after Truman's nomination, a group of Southern Democrats met in Alabama to nominate their own candidate for president, Governor Strom Thurmond, the arch-segregationist of South Carolina. They called their faction the States' Rights Party, but they were quickly nicknamed the Dixiecrats. Truman's party was now officially split.

It split again on July 27 when a group of party liberals nominated former vice president Henry Wallace, an original New Dealer, to be the candidate of the Progressive Party. The Democrats were split three ways, reminiscent of the party's bitter divisions in 1860, when Abraham Lincoln capitalized on

Democratic disarray to capture the presidency with less than 45 percent of the popular vote.

It was just a matter of time, it seemed, before the White House changed parties for the first time since 1933.

Truman crossed the nation by rail during the memorable 1948 campaign, delivering hundreds of speeches and giving his opponents hell.

CHAPTER 16

Giving Them Hell

Campaign Speech in St. Louis
October 30, 1948

TRACK 16

As Harry Truman suspected, the so-called Turnip Congress did nothing to advance the president's agenda, or its own, during a two-week special session in late July and early August. Truman asked Congress to act on some of the very issues cited in the Republican platform, such as inflation and housing. "We cannot afford to wait for the next Congress to act," Truman said.[1] Congress disagreed. With Truman's approval rating sitting at just 37 percent in the polls, Republican leaders saw no reason to pay much heed to a virtual lame-duck president.

Only in retrospect is it clear just how much of a blunder Republicans made by simply ignoring Truman's taunts and challenges. At the time, Harry Truman was considered as relevant as yesterday's news. Republican leaders convened the Congress as the president ordered, but they saw no reason to treat Harry Truman as anything more than a nuisance who would soon be sent home to Missouri and obscurity. All the polls showed that Thomas E. Dewey would be the next president; there was little reason for congressional Republicans to do anything but mop their brows—the Capitol building was not air-conditioned in the summer of 1948, and the weather was unbearably hot and humid—and then go home. Soon they would be done with the pesky, doomed Harry Truman.

Truman was prepared to pounce on the opposition's lethargy, but before he did, he showed that even a politically wounded president was not without power. On the very morning when lawmakers trudged into the Capitol for Day 1 of the Turnip Session, Harry Truman issued an executive order ending one of the nation's greatest injustices—the legal segregation of the U.S. armed forces. The Dixiecrats saw no reason to regret their split with Truman. Strom Thurmond, the Dixiecrats' presidential nominee, was asked why he refused to support Truman, whose rhetoric on civil rights was no different than Franklin Roosevelt's. "I agree," Thurmond said, "but Truman really means it."[2]

The campaign began in earnest on Friday morning, September 17, when Harry Truman boarded a special seventeen-car train called the Ferdinand Magellan. The train was specially outfitted for presidential travel, with armored plating, bulletproof glass, and first-class accommodations. Franklin Roosevelt used the train during his presidency, and now Harry Truman would take it on a thirty-three-day campaign swing that would cover nearly twenty-two thousand miles—a journey that would transform Harry Truman's political fortunes. Amazingly, the transformation would pass unnoticed by nearly everybody—except Harry Truman.

His running mate, Senator Alben Barkley, and his secretary of state, George Marshall, escorted Truman to the platform. Barkley, with his fog-horn voice, bellowed, "Mow 'em down, Harry." The president replied, "I'm going to fight hard. I'm going to give 'em hell."[3]

So began one of the most remarkable political campaigns in U.S. history. It was an extraordinary odyssey on many levels—logistically, it was a nightmare. The presidential train would have to pass through hundreds of grade crossings, any one of which posed a security threat. Truman needed to be in constant touch with the White House, for the Berlin airlift was ongoing and relations between Washington and Moscow were extremely tense. The Army Signal Corps built a communications car, which allowed the president to keep in touch with world events even as he spoke and waved and shook hands and did it all over again, every day for more than a month.

Meanwhile, an advance team worked to identify places where the presidential train would stop and Truman could deliver a speech from the rear platform of the Magellan's caboose. They recruited local officials—mayors, legislators, and other officials—to join the presidential train for short jaunts across the country. As for the candidate himself, he never displayed a moment of doubt or a hint of exhaustion. He seemed to relish the opportunity to speak his mind, and he did so in language that sounded very much like the language of everyday American life—not the Hudson Valley tones of Franklin Roosevelt or, for that matter, the careful, polished cadence of his opponent, Thomas Dewey. His attacks on his favorite target, the 80th Congress, dubbed the "do-nothing Congress," were ferocious, but Truman didn't spare voters who were thought to be wavering or apathetic. He chastised a group of farmers in Iowa, where voter turnout was light in the 1946 election that produced the 80th Congress. "You stayed at home in 1946," he said from the train platform, "and you got just exactly what you deserved. You didn't exercise your God-given right to control this country. Now you're going to have another chance."[4]

Most of his speeches were short—no more than five minutes, with five more minutes devoted to handshaking and other rituals before the train pulled away and set out for its next stop. Truman worked with a team of speechwriters, generally at night as they prepared for the next day's marathon campaigning. Clark Clifford, his assistant Charles Murphy, press secretary Charlie Ross, and others writers learned that the president liked to speak in simple declarative sentences. He spoke. He did not orate. That's what Thomas Dewey did. He reminded farmers in the Midwest that he, too, worked a plow; in fact, he was once told that he plowed the straightest furrow in the entire state of Missouri. Of course, the person who bestowed that honor on him, he admitted, was a little biased, as mothers tend to be.

Barely scripted and full of energy, Truman gleefully lambasted Republicans with colorful language that few incumbent presidents had ever used in describing their opponents. In Iowa, he accused Republicans of having "stuck a pitchfork in the farmer's back" by failing to back price supports.[5] During a stop in California, he charged that the Republicans wanted to "let the big fellows get the big incomes, and let a little of it trickle down off the table like the crumbs that fell to Lazarus."[6] Truman played the role of prairie populist like nobody since William Jennings Bryan, but as Truman knew well, William Jennings Bryan was (and remains) the only three-time loser in American history, having lost the presidential elections of 1896, 1900, and 1908. Bryan was revered for his golden voice, his lusty us-against-them rhetoric, and his inability to rally enough voters to win a general election.

Official Washington saw no reason to doubt that Truman was heading for a similar fate, even if there was pep in his speeches and even if he
was attracting thousands of people to his train as it snaked through Ohio,
Illinois, Iowa, Colorado, Utah, and California before it began its journey
back east. National correspondents were descending on Albany, the state
capital of New York, to report on future president Dewey's governing
style and prospective top aides. Dewey campaigned by train, with nearly
a hundred reporters tagging along, but there was little resemblance to the
hectic, spontaneous atmosphere aboard the Magellan. Dewey stuck to bland
generalities—calling for cooperation, and patriotism, and good government—while the media on board enjoyed the comforts of a first-class hotel
on wheels. The Dewey campaign even took care of reporters' laundry.

The Truman campaign, on the other hand, was unpredictable and ad
hoc, which many observers saw as further evidence of the administration's
incompetence. But the president's listeners seemed to enjoy Truman's
spontaneity and semi-scripted performances. At the end of each speech,
Truman brought out his wife, Bess, and daughter, Margaret, a gesture
that only added to each performance's charm. Word was starting to get
out: the feisty president was putting on a memorable show. Ten thousand
people heard him speak in San Diego. Several days later, on a Sunday
afternoon in San Antonio, two hundred thousand people cheered for the
president as he traveled by motorcade from the city's rail station to a
hotel, where he reminded listeners that he was a "servant of the people of
the United States."[7]

Truman spent four days campaigning through Texas, delivering two
dozen speeches to tens of thousands of listeners. He told crowds that
Democrats had to "fight isolationists and reactionaries, the profiteers and
the privileged class." Democrats, he said, sought to make sure that "the little
fellow gets a square deal." Republicans, on the other hand, were in league
with "the big money boys."[8] Dewey, who needed the support of people
who hadn't cast a vote for a Republican in twenty years, was careful not to
respond in kind about Democrats.

The tour continued, through Oklahoma and Kentucky, Illinois and
West Virginia. He spoke sixteen times on a single day, September 29,
and nine times the following day, when he left the train for a quick swing
through southern Illinois by car. The Magellan pulled into Union Station

on October 2 for a brief respite, allowing the president to catch up on the country's business, including a proposal, put together by two aides, to send Chief Justice Fred Vinson on a special mission to Moscow to negotiate an end to the Berlin blockade. The aides thought Truman needed a bold gesture to rescue his campaign, and while Truman supported the idea at first, he changed his mind when Secretary of State George Marshall objected.

If his aides thought the campaign needed an unorthodox gesture like the Vinson mission, Truman remained convinced that the tide was turning in his favor. On October 5, as he prepared to reboard the Magellan for a three-day swing through the Northeast, he dropped a line to his sister, Mary Jane Truman, reflecting on the long tour of September. "We made about a hundred and forty stops and I spoke over 147 times," he wrote. "We had tremendous crowds everywhere. From 6:30 in the morning until midnight the turnout was phenomenal. The news jerks didn't know what to make of it—so they just lied about it!"[9] Truman was not wrong in his assessment of the trip's news coverage. Most reporters dismissed the large crowds as mere curiosity seekers. The polls seemed to back up their skepticism: a Gallup poll released on September 24, halfway into Truman's cross-country tour, showed Dewey ahead of Truman by more than seven points.

Truman toured Philadelphia, Jersey City, Albany, and Buffalo in early October, and then set out on another long trip on October 10. Day one took him through the Republican stronghold of Ohio, where he delivered more than a dozen speeches on October 11. The train plowed through the heartland, through Indiana and then Illinois, where Truman was joined by Senate candidate Paul Douglas, who was astonished by what he saw. "There was great applause, and there were constant shouts of 'Give 'em hell, Harry,' and he was at home with the crowd," Douglas wrote. Truman connected with his listeners, Douglas noted, because he was "simple, unaffected, and determined."[10]

The same could not be said of his opponent, who was aware of the campaign's changing dynamics. A poll in mid-October found Truman trailing by just six points. In ordinary circumstances, a six-point lead with just a few weeks to go might seem comfortable. But Dewey and other Republicans knew this was no ordinary campaign. Harry Truman was campaigning like no other president had before, and he was making a difference. Dewey did nothing to slow Truman's momentum when he insulted the engineer of his campaign train during a rally in Illinois, when the train lurched slightly during the candidate's speech. He called the engineer a "lunatic" who "probably ought to be shot at sunrise."[11] Harry Truman, who cast himself as the champion of ordinary working people, could not have asked for better material from his opponent.

On October 30, with the election just three days away, Harry Truman prepared to wrap up his remarkable adventure. The Magellan took him from Ohio to Indiana to Illinois to, finally, his home state of Missouri, where he finished his typically long day with a set-piece speech in Kiel Auditorium in St. Louis. It was the last of 275 campaign speeches delivered in six eventful weeks. Like many of those speeches, this one veered from the script and was filled with colorful denunciations of Republicans in general and the 80th Congress in particular.

He began with a reflection on the great events that marked the first few months of his sudden and unexpected tenure as Franklin Roosevelt's successor—he reminded his audience of the Allied victory over Germany, the surrender of Japan, the founding of the United Nations, and the beginning of a new, postwar era of prosperity. By implication, he contrasted his years of decision making with the deliberations of the "Republican 'do-nothing' Congress," which stood for "special interests" and employed columnists and radio commentators to smear him. Truman's anger was directed not only at the stock villains of his campaign—the Republicans in Congress—but also against media barons, whom he mentioned by name. There were the "character assassins" of the Hearst chain and the "saboteurs" in the employ of Richard McCormick and Robert Patterson, who ran the *Chicago Tribune*, a powerful Republican voice in the Midwest.

After citing statistic after statistic to remind listeners how much better off they were in 1948 than they were in 1933—a subtle way of running against the Republican Party of Herbert Hoover—Truman told his audience that they had an obligation to the Democratic Party. They had stood aside in 1946, he said, and allowed Republicans to elect the 80th Congress. "Most laboring men stayed away from the polls in 1946, and see what they got! They got the Taft-Hartley Act." If they stayed home again, he said, they deserved a similar fate.

Why they would stay home was a mystery, for, as he saw it, progress and prosperity were at risk on Election Day. With that, he launched into attack mode. "Of all the fake campaigns, this one is the tops, so far as the Republican candidate for president is concerned," Truman said. He had been careful in his remarks about Dewey, preferring to rail against the institutional Republican Party and its nameless leaders in Congress. But with polls tightening, Truman decided to bring Dewey into the debate, although he didn't mention him by name. "He has been following me up and down this country making speeches about home and mother and unity and efficiency, and things of that kind. He won't talk about the issues, but he did let his foot slip when he endorsed the 80th Congress." Truman feigned disbelief. "He endorsed that Congress! He said that Congress had done great things for the future of this country."

That Congress, he said, passed a "rich man's tax bill" that cut taxes on people "getting $100,000 a year," a salary, he noted, that was "four times the net salary of the president of the United States." He called another Republican tax-cut proposal "one of the most terrible political documents ever I saw."

He wanted better pay for teachers, smaller class sizes, and a health-insurance program, but Republicans weren't interested and their allies in the press gave them aid and comfort. Truman shrewdly cast aspersions on newspaper coverage of his campaign, suggesting that the confident predictions of a Dewey administration were based not on voter sentiment but on the media's pro-Republican bias. "Now, my friends," he said, "I have been all over these United States from one end to another, and when I started out the song was, well, you can't win, the Democrats can't win. Ninety percent of the press is against us, but that didn't discourage me one bit. You know, I had four campaigns here in the great state of Missouri, and I never had a metropolitan paper for me that whole time. And I licked them every time!"

It happened before, and, Truman predicted, it would happen again. "People are waking up to the fact that this is their government, and that they can control their government if they get out and vote on election day. That is all they need to do."

Truman never seemed to doubt that if he could get people to the polls, they would do the right thing by him. But pre-election polls still found him trailing Dewey by about five points. The newspapers in late October were not terribly interested in Harry Truman's pathetic attempts to rally the troops. Instead, they began setting the stage for the first Republican president since Hoover.

After Truman left the stage in St. Louis, he headed to his home town of Independence. "I returned from the bedlam of the longest and hardest political campaign of my career," he wrote, "to the restful quiet of my home."[12]

Few believed he had any reason to expect much more than "restful quiet" for the rest of his days.

Harry Truman, his running mate Alben Barkley, and their families celebrate their unlikely victory in 1948.

CHAPTER 17

Truman Defeats Dewey

Victory Speech in Independence, Missouri
November 3, 1948

TRACK 17

T HE ERA OF FRANKLIN ROOSEVELT WAS ABOUT TO COME TO A SPECTACULAR
end. The coalition over which he presided was shattered, in part
because his successor simply was in over his head, incapable of
pulling off the shrewd juggling act that had kept Southern segregationists
in league with Northern liberals, Protestants in cahoots with Catholics and
Jews, laborers in alliance with intellectuals. Harry Truman, the accidental
president, may have shown admirable courage and determination during
an exhausting campaign, but he was doomed—a parochial, narrow man
who simply could not fill the shoes of his illustrious predecessor.

The nation's newspapers—the most important source of information
for most voters in 1948—did little to disguise their conviction that scrappy
Harry Truman was about to suffer an historic rejection at the polls. The
New York Times forecast that Thomas E. Dewey would win 345 electoral
votes while Truman would win just 105, with the rest—38—going to
Dixiecrat Strom Thurmond. Magazines, trying to stay ahead of the story,
offered forward-looking pieces about the future Dewey administration.
Policy analysts fretted about the coming transition between Truman and
Dewey—who would be in charge between Election Day and Inauguration
Day, they wondered.

It wasn't just reporters who were sure that the election was over before the first vote was cast. James Maloney decided that his place on Election Day was with Governor Dewey—Maloney was the director of the Secret Service, the agency in charge of protecting the president's personal security.

At 9:37 p.m. on November 1, 1948, Harry Truman delivered an election-eve radio broadcast to the nation from his house—actually, his mother-in-law's house—at 219 North Delaware Street in Independence. At this late hour, with the nation's leading opinion makers certain that the president's vigorous campaign was in vain, Truman displayed the same sharp-edged populist rhetoric that had won over crowds across the country. "Tomorrow you will be deciding between the principles of the Democratic Party—the party of the people—and the principles of the Republican Party—the party of privilege," he said. He made no mention of Franklin Roosevelt, but he was careful to remind voters of the "dark days of 1932." Those days, he said, could never be repeated.[1]

The next morning, Election Day, started like just about every other morning in Independence. Harry Truman was awake before dawn, as he always was, and as was his custom, he took a morning constitutional. Later in the morning, the president, first lady, and daughter Margaret walked to their local polling place, Memorial Hall, a few blocks from their home. He had lunch with some friends at the Rockwood Country Club and told reporters that he was certain of victory.

In New York, Dewey rose after nine o'clock in the Roosevelt Hotel in midtown Manhattan, had lunch, and traveled by limousine to cast his vote. Enthusiastic New Yorkers, who had had one of their own as president from 1933 to 1945, cheered their governor as he and his wife emerged from their car on East 51st Street to cast their votes in a local public school. Smiling and confident, Dewey acknowledged the crowd's cheers. A homemade sign on a nearby building read: "Good luck, Mr. President."[2]

As millions of Americans cast their own votes, the president of the United States decided he wanted to be alone as his fellow citizens decided his fate. As dusk descended on Missouri, Truman asked his Secret Service entourage to take him to a resort called The Elms in the small Missouri town of Excelsior Springs, thirty miles outside Kansas City. As Truman biographer David McCullough noted, Truman had been to The Elms sixteen years earlier, after his friend and mentor, political boss Tom Pendergast, decided against endorsing Truman for governor of Missouri. Truman tried to put his disappointment behind him back then; now, he sought quiet and tranquility as he awaited America's decision.

Truman monitored the returns in his room, alone. He dined on a ham and cheese sandwich and listened to the radio as early results poured in. Dewey was ahead in the east, which many commentators took as a sign of things to come. Truman decided to get some sleep at nine o'clock, as crowds began to gather outside his home in Independence. The well-wishers, of course, had no idea that the president wasn't inside.

As midnight approached, radio commentators were reporting that Truman was ahead in the popular vote nationwide, but few believed the trend would last. One of the era's most famous radio journalists, H. V. Kaltenborn, asserted that there simply was no way Harry Truman could hold onto his lead. Truman woke up just in time to hear Kaltenborn's assurances. The president drifted back to sleep, but awoke again at about four o'clock. Again, he turned on the radio to hear Kaltenborn. This time, the commentator was reporting that Truman was ahead by two million votes, but, Kaltenborn said, Dewey still looked like a winner. Truman left The Elms at six in the morning, convinced that Kaltenborn was wrong. Not everybody was so certain. At some point in the early hours of November 3, editors of the *Chicago Tribune* wrote a headline destined to become a piece of history—although not the sort of history the editors would have liked. Early editions of the *Tribune* proclaimed: "Dewey Defeats Truman."

The Secret Service drove Truman to a hotel in Kansas City, where his exhausted staff had worked through the night, their anxiety giving way to hope and, now, to joy. Their man continued to hold his lead as dawn broke. He was ahead in the Midwest. Thurmond had managed to win only four states in the South. The president changed his clothes, shaved, and joined his staff as results continued to dribble in. His calm demeanor amazed his aides—the greatest political upset in American presidential history was unfolding before their eyes, but Harry Truman seemed to be unsurprised. It was as though he was expecting this result all the while.

Mid-morning brought news that Truman carried Ohio, clinching a majority in the Electoral College. Soon there was more good news: Democrats gained control of both houses of Congress. Truman's flaying of the 80th Congress had worked its magic.

Thomas Dewey conceded the race just after eleven o'clock. He sent Truman a telegram of congratulations and called on the country to rally behind him. Two hours later, Dewey met with reporters in New York. "I was just as surprised as you are," he told the press, noting that he had "read your stories before the election." He expressed no regrets, saying only that he had enjoyed the campaign "immensely."[3]

Crowds began to gather in Harry Truman's home town in the late afternoon. By eight o'clock, some forty thousand people were gathered in the courthouse square in Independence, near the office where Harry Truman toiled as an obscure county judge so many years earlier. They were on hand to witness history: a victory speech from one of American history's most unlikely victors, a man who happened to be a neighbor.

Harry Truman, wearing a light, double-breasted suit, stood on the courthouse steps, between two large columns and in front of a battery of microphones. It was dark, so the courthouse was bathed in harsh white lights. Men and women inside the courthouse looked down at Truman from second-story windows.

If the president displayed little emotion hours earlier, when the results were official, he was not so reluctant now. Beaming, he addressed himself first to the town's mayor, Roger T. Sermon. "I want to inform you, Mr. Mayor, that protocol goes out the window when I am in Independence," he said. "I am a citizen of this town, and a taxpayer, and I want to be treated just like the rest of the taxpayers in this community are treated." The crowd roared, prompting Truman to say that the celebration was "not for me. It is for the whole country. It is for the whole world, for the simple reason that you have given me a tremendous responsibility."

The election of 1948, the first presidential election of the postwar era, came as the United States carved out a place for itself in world affairs as never before. Truman implicitly acknowledged that, asking his country-men for their help in ensuring "the welfare of this great republic" and the "welfare and peace of the world at large."

He promised to "carry out the Democratic platform," a task which would be a good deal easier than in the past, thanks to Republican losses throughout the country. "And we have a Congress now," he said, "and I am sure we will make some progress in the next four years." And with that, he thanked his neighbors—all forty thousand of them—and basked in their cheers.

The following day, as he traveled by train to Washington, Truman gave another victory speech in St. Louis. There, while addressing a crowd at Union Station, he held up a copy of the *Chicago Tribune* with its huge headline: "Dewey Defeats Truman." Photographers captured the moment, and the image became a symbol of Harry Truman's improbable victory in 1948.

In the end, Truman polled 24.1 million votes to Dewey's 21.9 million. He captured 303 electoral votes, while Dewey won 189 and Thurmond, 39. Raw numbers do little justice to just how close the election was—Truman won Ohio by about 7,000 votes, and California by just 17,000. On the other hand, the third-party candidacies of Strom Thurmond and Henry Wallace did not drain large numbers of votes from Truman as many suspected they would.

The election was not only historic. It was a personal triumph for the man from Independence who never seemed to consider defeat an option. He arrived back in Washington at three o'clock in the morning on November 5. Well-wishers by the hundreds of thousands were on hand to greet the president and his party. A banner flew from the headquarters of the *Washington Post*, reading: "Mr. President, we are ready to eat crow whenever you are ready to serve it."

On November 7, the president left Washington for a well-deserved vacation in Key West. He did very little for two weeks, in part because he knew that the next four years promised to be no less eventful than the previous four.

PART THREE:
A Term of His Own, 1949–1953

In his second term, Harry Truman became a wartime president again as he sent U.S. troops to Korea to defend against Communist aggression.

Introduction

FOREIGN AFFAIRS DOMINATED THE NEXT FOUR YEARS OF HARRY TRUMAN'S presidency, as the United States consolidated its unprecedented leadership in global affairs. Gone for good were the voices of isolation with which Truman's predecessor, Franklin Roosevelt, fought so furiously through the 1930s and into the early '40s. Truman presided over the shaping of a bipartisan consensus on foreign policy designed to rebuild the nations of Western Europe, defend friendly governments from internal or external threats, and halt the spread of Communism. Even the most dramatic domestic crisis of Truman's term, a threatened strike in the nation's steel mills, was seen as a threat not to harmony at home, but national security abroad, for the nation's armed services depended on steel production.

Truman enjoyed success and popular approval for his European policy, as the rebuilding of allies and onetime foes continued to achieve remarkable results. The nations of the North Atlantic came together to form a collective security alliance known as the North Atlantic Treaty Organization, binding each member to the defense of its allies. For the United States, this venture into collective security was yet another historical step away from the isolation of the past. Truman continued to pledge full support to another progressive venture in collective security, the United Nations.

In Asia, however, the White House found itself on the defensive. A long civil war in China ended with a Communist victory, which Republicans, including a young congressman from California named Richard Nixon, blamed on the White House. Anxiety about Communist gains around the world inspired Senator Joseph McCarthy of Wisconsin to charge that Communist agents had infiltrated the administration, and that Truman's top aides were dupes—if not outright spies and traitors. At first Truman believed McCarthy could be ignored because his charges were so reckless, his behavior so erratic. He soon reconsidered, and complained bitterly that top Republicans refused to rebut McCarthy's slanders against respected public servants like former Secretary of State General George C. Marshall.

The gravest crisis of the new term came in July 1950, when the Communist government of North Korea invaded South Korea, an ally of the West. The United States persuaded the United Nations to come to the defense of the South, with American forces providing most of the manpower. Under the command of war hero General Douglas MacArthur, the UN forces pushed back the invaders, but the war became immensely more complicated when Communist China entered the war to assist the North. Disagreements over strategy led Truman to remove MacArthur from command.

Korea cast a long shadow over the remainder of Truman's tenure. The war settled into an unpopular stalemate, and Truman's approval ratings fell dramatically. He announced in early 1952 that he would not be a candidate for reelection. His handpicked choice as the Democratic Party's nominee, Adlai Stevenson, lost to Dwight Eisenhower in the fall, ending a twenty-year Democratic monopoly on the presidency.

Truman retired to Independence with Bess. He settled into the role of elder statesman until he began to falter in the late 1960s. He died in 1972 at the age of eighty-eight.

Against all odds and expectations (except his own), Harry Truman
took the oath of office for a second time on January 20, 1949.

CHAPTER 18

The Four Points

Inaugural Address
January 20, 1949

TRACK 18

T HROUGH MOST OF 1948, MANY AMERICANS HAD BEEN LED TO BELIEVE THAT the new year, 1949, would bring dramatic change. Of course, the change some people (although clearly not everybody) anticipated did not take place—the man at the head of the U.S. government remained the same. But the place he and his family called home, the White House, was in desperate need of change. The place was falling apart. Shortly after the president's return from Key West, he learned from federal architects and other experts that the iconic building was simply uninhabitable. A massive and immediate renovation was required. The Trumans would have to live elsewhere while the mansion was gutted and fixed, although the president would be able to continue to work in the West Wing during the renovation.

The Trumans packed up and moved across Pennsylvania Avenue to the Blair House, where they had lived briefly after Franklin Roosevelt's death while they gave his widow, Eleanor, time to collect herself and her belongings. The change in living arrangements did not seem to affect the president, although he found the new digs more crowded than the old place. "It is a nice place," he wrote, "but only half as large—so we have no place to put guests."[1] He even managed to find a bright side to the hastened move across the street. It was a shame, he said, that "the old White House had to fall down." But it was a good thing, he added, that it didn't fall down during a reception, when as many as 1,500 people could have been inside.[2]

The Secret Service could not have been so sanguine about the change. They fretted that Blair House lacked the green buffer areas and fences of the White House. The president of the United States would come and go through a door that led directly to a sidewalk—the notion of simply rerouting traffic away from Blair House was either not considered or disregarded. Making matters even less secure, Truman's bedroom windows faced the street. The good news for the Secret Service was that the repairs to the White House were expected to take no more than a year. Truman hoped to have personal control over the project, but Congress insisted in appointing a committee to oversee the work instead.

The renovation wasn't finished until March 1952.

Harry Truman's cabinet also underwent an important structural change as 1949 dawned. Secretary of State George C. Marshall, the man Harry Truman revered as a national hero, resigned in early January. Marshall was ailing and was scheduled to have a kidney removed; Truman accepted his resignation with reluctance. The president replaced Marshall with Dean Acheson, who would go on to become one of the main architects of Washington's Cold War policy during Truman's new term.

As Truman prepared to take the oath of office for a second time—this time under very different and far happier circumstances than the first—he went to Capitol Hill on January 5 to deliver a State of the Union message that offered an outline of his domestic agenda for the next four years. "We have rejected the discredited theory that the fortunes of the nation should be in the hands of the privileged few," he said. "We have abandoned the 'trickle-down' concept of national prosperity. Instead, we believe that our economic system should rest on a democratic foundation and that wealth should be created for the benefit of all. The recent election shows that the people of the United States are in favor of this kind of society and want to go on improving it."[3]

He asked Congress to repeal the Taft-Hartley Act, urged more federal financial assistance for education, proposed a federal plan to clear slums and build low-rent public housing, and demanded an increase in Social Security payments. "Every segment of our population and every individual has a right to expect from our government a fair deal," he said. The phrase stuck—Truman's domestic agenda, which included national health insurance and other liberal reforms, became known in the press as the "Fair Deal." Truman told Congress that domestic policy and foreign policy were inseparable because, he said, the world looked to the United States since it enjoyed "the benefits of democratic government for which most of the peoples of the world are yearning." Democracy and justice at home, he said, would serve as a beacon for those who yearned for freedom abroad.

As Inauguration Day approached, Truman, his advisors—including his new secretary of state—and his speechwriters surveyed the state of the world as Truman prepared to deliver the first substantive inaugural address since Franklin Roosevelt's third in 1941 (Roosevelt's fourth, delivered in 1945, was just a few hundred words, part of a deliberately low-key wartime ceremony). At first Truman was inclined to stick to his domestic agenda in his inaugural, but aides, including speechwriter George Elsey, persuaded him that domestic politics were best suited for State of the Union messages. An inaugural address, Elsey argued, was intended for the world and was designed to send a signal to friend and foe alike. The inaugural address of 1949 would be like no other in U.S. history, for Washington had never been so powerful and had never been in such a position to dictate the world's agenda. Elsey convinced Truman that the inaugural should be designed as a statement of foreign policy.

To be sure, there was plenty to remind Truman and his staff that the world demanded their attention. The United States was technically at peace but nevertheless engaged in a quasi-conflict with a nation, the Soviet Union, and an ideology, international Communism. U.S. planes continued to deliver food and other necessities to the besieged citizens of West Berlin, cut off from the rest of the world by Red Army troops who refused to allow traffic in and out of the city. Thousands of miles away, Washington's wartime ally in China, Chiang Kai-shek, fought an increasingly desperate battle with Communist insurgents led by Mao Zedong. The prospect of Communist governments in Moscow and Beijing frightened American policymakers and military leaders. Just as frightening, perhaps even more so, was the prospect of Communists in Washington. A top official in the State Department, Alger Hiss, was accused of being a Soviet spy and was under indictment for lying to Congress. As Truman and his writers drafted an inaugural speech designed for a worldwide audience and crafted as the mission statement of the world's greatest power, they were increasingly concerned about the ambitions of their former allies in Moscow, and *their* allies around the world.

Inauguration day 1949 was cold but clear and sunny, a brilliant winter's morning. Truman was up and out of Blair House before dawn to keep a breakfast appointment with some old friends—his Army buddies from Battery D, 129th Field Artillery, who were holding a reunion in the Mayflower Hotel in his honor. The president, dressed in a business suit, shook hands with his comrades, who knew him as "Captain Harry" long before he became commander in chief. At 7:45 a.m., Truman rose to deliver a short speech, during which he told his comrades in arms that they would have a place of honor in the inaugural parade later that day. There was a catch, however. He told them that he expected them to march at a pace of 120 steps per minute—the pace he kept during his morning constitutionals. Truman was one of the older men in Battery D, but the younger men in the crowd rolled their eyes and groaned when they heard this presidential order. It wasn't that they were completely out of shape, but many had been awake and celebrating for hours.

When Truman mentioned the pace he expected from his men, one of them came forward and presented the president with a walking stick. He was delighted. "That is a beautiful walking stick," he said. "I use one every morning. I was intending to walk up here this morning, but I was afraid to wear out the newspaper correspondents, so I came in a car!" He took another look at the stick, and said it was "something that my daughter can perhaps some day give to my grandson."[4] Somewhere in the audience, twenty-four-year-old Margaret Truman must have been blushing. (Her first child, a son, was not born until 1957.)

After the Trumans left the Mayflower, they returned to the White House—the relatively safe West Wing—in preparation for the more formal ceremonies. The president traded in his business suit for a top hat, formal jacket, and trousers. They prayed at St. John's Episcopal Church and then, with incoming Vice President Alben Barkley, they drove to Capitol Hill, where a vast, jubilant crowd awaited them.

More people would see the president of the United States take the oath of office this morning than ever before, thanks to the new mass medium of television. Truman's was the first inaugural ceremony covered on television, although the primitive technology meant that only those living east of the Mississippi River could tune in. The signal from Washington went only so far in 1949. About 100 million people followed the ceremony using the old, reliable medium of radio.

He began speaking at about 1:30, an hour and a half after his old term had expired. Bareheaded—he took off his top hat to take the oath of office—and serious, Truman said he accepted the burdens of office "with a resolve to do all I can for the welfare of this nation and for the peace of the world."

To casual listeners, whether they were gathered in front of him or gathered in front of televisions and radios, the speech sounded like an eloquent argument on behalf of democratic systems under threat from totalitarian Communism. "Communism is based on the belief that man is so weak and inadequate that he is unable to govern himself, and therefore requires the rule of strong masters," he said. "Democracy is based on the conviction that man has the moral and intellectual capacity, as well as the inalienable right, to govern himself with reason and justice." Communism, he continued, suppressed dissent, regarded violence as just another political tactic, and saw the world in perpetual conflict. Democracy, on the other hand, sought consensus, achieved justice without violence, and viewed government as an instrument on behalf of the individual. The speech was, indeed, a Cold War document, with no overt domestic content. But a careful reading of the speech, and Truman read it carefully, revealed the ways in which Truman linked his domestic agenda to his foreign policy priorities.

The speech quickly became known as the Point Four speech, for it outlined four ways in which his administration planned to counter the Communist threat around the world. "First," he said, "we will continue to give unfaltering support to the United Nations and related agencies, and we will continue to search for ways to strengthen their authority and increase their effectiveness." While not a particularly remarkable assertion, Truman's first point effectively put an end to any lingering doubts about America's support for the UN and its willingness to assume global responsibilities. His second point was a renewed commitment to the Marshall Plan for the reconstruction of Europe, now well underway. "Third," he said, "we will strengthen freedom-loving nations against the dangers of aggression." He hinted that a new agreement for collective security in the North Atlantic was under negotiation. Collective security, he said, was critical in an age of ideological warfare.

Truman's fourth point caught his informed listeners off guard, and represented a melding of sort of his domestic priorities—the Fair Deal—and his foreign policy agenda. "Fourth," he said, "we must embark on a bold new program for making the benefits of our scientific advances and industrial progress available for the improvement and growth of underdeveloped areas."

Just a few weeks earlier, in his State of the Union message, Truman spoke passionately about Americans who lacked decent medical care and access to quality schools. Now, he addressed those concerns on a global scale, arguing that Washington had a role in easing the plight of the poor abroad, just as it had an obligation to the poor at home. "More than half the people of the world are living in conditions approaching misery," he said. "Their food is inadequate. They are victims of disease. Their economic life is primitive and stagnant."

The United States, he contended, should assist poor, peace-loving nations to become more productive for the good of all their citizens. "Our aim should be to help the free peoples of the world, through their own efforts, to produce more food, more clothing, more materials for housing, and more mechanical power to lighten their burdens."

The goal, he said, was not to expand American power, but to lift other human beings out of poverty and deprivation. "The old imperialism—exploitation for foreign profit—has no place in our plans," he said. "What we envisage is a program of development based on the concepts of democratic fair dealing." The phrase fairly echoed his description of his domestic agenda—the implementation of a fair deal for all people. Such an agenda would foster freedom and democracy and, not coincidentally, foil the plans of those seen to be freedom's enemies.

Truman's fourth point was the most eloquent and visionary portion of the speech, but the one that would be the most difficult to implement. Congress was not so enthusiastic about sharing the nation's resources, and this point remained an ideal, not a plan, until John F. Kennedy adapted it as a mission statement for the Peace Corps in 1961.

Truman signs a treaty creating the North Atlantic Treaty Organization, another attempt at collective security for the United States and its allies.

CHAPTER 19

"A Simple Document"

Creation of the NATO Alliance
April 4, 1949

TRACK 19

N O AMERICAN ADMINISTRATION HAD ENTERED INTO A MILITARY ALLIANCE SINCE George Washington took the oath of office for the first time in 1789. Although it was not Washington, but Thomas Jefferson, who warned the country against "entangling alliances," Washington's wariness of the Old World framed American foreign policy from the late eighteenth century to the middle of the twentieth century—the so-called "American Century." American isolationists who successfully opposed U.S. membership in the League of Nations, and who less successfully sought to keep the United States out of World War II, claimed to be the inheritors of Washington's legacy.

The world was a good deal smaller in 1949 than it was in 1789, or in 1919. Long-range bombers, missiles, submarines, and other modern weapons of mass destruction did not respect the once vast spaces that separated the United States from Europe and Asia. What's more, in the global village that emerged after World War II, the United States gained a new appreciation for the values it shared with portions of the Old World. Americans fought side by side with Britain and France in two world wars, and while the two aging colonial powers had their differences with Washington, the fight against Nazi totalitarianism allowed all sides to step back and examine what they had in common, rather than obsess over what divided them.

President Truman, who fought in France during the latter stages of World War I, believed that America's security was inextricably linked to the security of liberal democracies in Western Europe, most prominently Britain and France, as well as America's neighbor to the north, Canada. Whatever their differences of culture, tradition, and economics, these nations believed in and practiced democratic values. Those who opposed or threatened democracy were not the enemies of a single nation-state, but of all democratic nations.

In the late 1940s, such an enemy existed: the Soviet Union, the one-time ally of the Western democracies. The Soviet-inspired overthrow of Czechoslovakia's democratically elected government in 1948 and the installation of pro-Soviet governments in Poland and Hungary worsened relations between East and West. "To the plain people of Europe, who were just beginning to take courage from the Marshall Plan, these Communist moves looked the beginning of a Russian 'big push,'" Truman wrote.[1] The great cities of Europe were only just beginning to rebuild, and the graves of millions of soldiers and civilians were only freshly dug. The prospect of yet another conflict was far too horrible to contemplate. But as the democratically elected leader of the most powerful nation on earth, Truman had no choice but to dwell on the unthinkable.

He had been doing so for some time. During his memorable campaign in 1948, even as he attacked Republicans in Congress for favoring a return to prewar isolation, he worked with Republican Senator Arthur Vandenberg to win overwhelming Senate approval of a resolution supporting a defense policy based on regional cooperation and assistance. Truman saw the vote as the first step toward a broader U.S. security policy, one that would not stop at the shores of the Atlantic and Pacific Oceans.

Western Europeans, all too familiar with the politics of alliance and balance of power, were already moving toward collective security as a defense against yet another disastrous war. Britain, France, Belgium, the Netherlands, and Luxembourg were already in conversation about mutual defense treaties against an attack from the East. These conversations helped lay the groundwork for a broad conception of Western Europe as a bulwark against totalitarianism and aggression, and as the incubator of liberal values.

The five nations signed an agreement, called the Brussels Pact, which pledged that all would come to the aid of one in the case of an attack.

In the spring of 1948, British Foreign Minister Ernest Bevin approached Washington about the possibility of forming a transatlantic alliance that would include the United States and Canada as well as the nations of northwest Europe. The proposed alliance was clearly designed as collective protection against a Soviet attack, but there was a political calculation as well. The French remained dubious about American plans to rebuild western Germany—after all, Germany had invaded France twice within a quarter-century. A multinational commitment to the defense of the West, Bevin told Truman, would ease France's concerns about Germany's reconstruction.

With the Senate's support for a broader approach to national defense, the Truman administration entered into negotiations in London with the five members of the Brussels Pact during the summer of 1948. "These conversations were held in the utmost secrecy," Truman wrote. "Special couriers handled all papers. Telephone conversation of matters covered in the conference was absolutely ruled out, and telegraphic communication was held to a minimum."[2] During these talks, the phrase "North Atlantic pact" came into common usage, further suggesting a military alliance that would not only cross borders, but an ocean as well.

The London talks were filled with obstacles and conflicting agendas. France, for example, wished to include its colonial possessions in North Africa as part of the fledgling mutual defense alliance. For Americans, a constitutional issue emerged—the Europeans wanted all parties to commit to going to war if an alliance partner came under attack. U.S. diplomats, however, pointed out that only Congress could declare war, and only after at least a semblance of debate. Canadian diplomats suggested compromise language that committed all partners to consider an attack on an ally as an attack on each member of the alliance. The wording did not commit members to war, but did commit them to considering an attack on another sovereign nation as an attack on itself. For the United States, this was a precedent-shattering venture into a global, multinational alliance. It would mean that an attack on Paris or London would be considered an attack on Washington, an extraordinary thought for a nation that had entered World War II only after an attack on its home territory. (Britain and France, of course, declared war on Germany in 1939 after the German invasion of

Poland, long before German soldiers set foot in France, long before German bombers assaulted the British homeland.)

Ironically, as the conferees discussed the importance of mutual security in the face of possible Soviet aggression, the place where tensions were highest—Berlin—was fairly tranquil, all things considered. The Soviets continued their blockade, and the Americans continued to resupply the western portion of the city by air. But neither side issued any threats or engaged in any provocative actions. Historian Marc Trachtenberg noted that the Soviets declined to jam radar signals essential to the airlift's successes, and Soviet officials actually cooperated with American and British authorities in monitoring air routes leading into the city.[3]

The London talks led, in September 1948, to an agreement that a transatlantic security treaty ought to be negotiated.[4] Plans were put on hold during the campaign, but after Truman's reelection, negotiations resumed in earnest. American enthusiasm for collective security was such that it pushed for a broader geographic and strategic approach—the Truman administration pushed for the inclusion of Italy, not exactly an Atlantic nation-state but, in Washington's view, an important bulwark against the Soviets. The roster of potential allies expanded to include the truly Atlantic nations of Norway, Denmark, Iceland, and Portugal. Not included, however, was the fledgling new state of West Germany, still under Allied occupation. The Germans had not yet made the transition from vanquished foe to reliable ally in the new East-West confrontation. The thought of a revived German military was frightening enough in 1949; the notion of an armed Germany in alliance with Britain, France, and the United States was, for some, still unthinkable. Still, West Germany was a critical piece of geography in the new strategic map of Europe—its integration into the new alliance was inevitable.

Diplomats and military chiefs spent the winter and early spring of 1949 working on a new treaty that would link Europe and North America together for the first time. The proposed alliance not only pledged each member to common defense, but also provided for a sharing of facilities like air bases and some standardization of military equipment and training. The treaty was ready for signatures on April 4, 1949. Representatives of twelve nations gathered in Washington for a signing ceremony and to hear President Truman proclaim the birth of the North Atlantic Treaty Organization, America's first military alliance since the end of the Revolution.

Truman arrived at the State Department's headquarters in Washington in late afternoon. Dressed in a dark suit and hat, a jaunty white handkerchief neatly folded in the left pocket of his jacket, Truman smiled as the flashbulbs of news photographers lit up his face. He proceeded to an auditorium where his secretary of state, Dean Acheson, and the foreign ministers of the other eleven signatory nations awaited him.

In his very first sentence, his greeting to the assembled foreign ministers, Truman signaled the formal end of centuries of American foreign policy and the beginning of something new. "I am happy," he said, "to welcome the foreign ministers of the countries which, together with the United States, form the North Atlantic community of nations." With those words, Truman acknowledged the new reality of American policy—the United States was no longer an island onto itself, no longer a nation living in splendid isolation. It was part of a larger community, a community that included the nations of the Old World, nations that America's founders looked upon with deep suspicion.

Truman was aware of the moment and its importance. With a Roosevelt-like touch for the homey metaphor, he explained to his larger audience—the American people—why the new alliance was important. "What we are about to do here is a neighborly act," he said, taking the edge off a document designed to thwart the presumed ambitions of the Soviets. "We are like a group of householders, living in the same locality, who decide to express their community of interests by entering into a formal association for their mutual self-protection."

They were gathered to sign what he called "a simple document." All it required was a commitment to the "peaceful principles of the United Nations, to maintain friendly relations and economic cooperation with one another, to consult together whenever the territory or independence of any of them is threatened, and to come to the aid of any one of them who may be attacked."

Contained in those simple phrases, however, was an historic commitment to peace and mutual defense. Truman argued that if the new North Atlantic Treaty had been in effect in 1914 or 1939, the world might have been spared two world wars that took the lives of tens of millions, civilians and soldiers alike. Military aggressors, he suggested, would not have dared attack nations that were part of a multilateral mutual-defense alliance.

Truman framed the NATO alliance as a means to achieving the UN's promise of peaceful cooperation among nations. Alliance members, he said, would conduct their affairs in accordance with the UN charter. "There are those who claim that this treaty is an aggressive act on the part of the nations which ring the North Atlantic," Truman said. "That is absolutely untrue. The pact will be a positive, not a negative, influence for peace, and its influence will be felt not only in the area it specifically covers but throughout the world." He again held out the specter of global conflict, insisting that the treaty was a step forward for peace, a move to ensure that the tragedies of 1914 and 1939 would not happen again. "Our peoples, to whom our governments are responsible, demand that these things shall not happen again," he said.

That required, in an era of global conflict, a global commitment to collective security among nations that shared democratic values, even if they applied those values in different ways. "We believe that it is possible for nations to achieve unity on the great principles of human freedom and justice, and at the same time to permit, in other respects, the greatest diversity of which the human mind is capable," he said. Those who doubted such a vision need only look to the United States, he added, where a diverse population created a united nation devoted to the shared principles of justice, democracy, and liberty.

While he was careful to avoid mention of the Soviet Union or of Communism, while he sought to frame the North Atlantic Treaty as a vehicle for peace, Truman did not resist the opportunity to contrast the new alliance with the values of other nations. "This method of organizing diverse people and cultures is in direct contrast to the method of the police state, which attempts to achieve unity by imposing the same beliefs and the same rule of force on everyone," he said.

The world, he suggested, was divided between those who would choose freedom and those who would choose slavery. Those who were about to sign their names to the North Atlantic Treaty had made their decision, he said, and acted accordingly.

After the president spoke and the treaty was signed, Truman and the dignitaries retired to a reception in the Carlton Hotel nearby. Truman proposed a toast: "We have really passed a milestone in history," he announced.

The North Atlantic Treaty Organization survived the Cold War, expanded into Eastern Europe after the fall of the Soviet Union, and coordinated an air war against aggression in the Balkans in the 1990s. Its mutual-defense provisions were enacted only once—after terrorists attacked the United States on September 11, 2001.

The Truman administration sought to prop up the regime
of Chinese nationalist leader Chiang Kai-shek, but he was
forced to flee to Taiwan.

CHAPTER 20

The Cornerstone of Peace

Address at the New United Nations Headquarters
October 24, 1949

TRACK 20

O N MAY 12, 1949, LIFE RETURNED TO NORMAL AGAIN IN WEST BERLIN. ROADS to the city were reopened, allowing trucks to deliver goods as they did in any other city. Fourteen months after the first U.S. airplane delivered supplies to West Berliners from the air, the Soviet Union conceded defeat in its effort to push its former allies out of their island garrison behind the Iron Curtain.

The U.S. Air Force flew more than a quarter-million missions over the city, dropping 2.3 million tons of food and supplies. It was a display of determination, restraint, and courage that lifted the spirits of the West in general, and the Truman White House in particular. Soviet Communism seemed to be on the march in the late 1940s, overtaking Eastern Europe and threatening nations like Italy, France, and Greece. On the other side of the world, in China, a Communist insurgency continued to gain ground against America's allies, the nationalist Chinese. Victory over West Berlin allowed Harry Truman and his foreign-policy team to take credit for a significant, bloodless victory over Communist provocation. "When we refused to be forced out of the city of Berlin," Truman wrote, "we demonstrated to the people of Europe that with their cooperation we would act, and act resolutely, when their freedom was threatened. Politically it brought the peoples of Western Europe more closely to us."[1]

But Truman had little time to bask in his hard-earned victory. Just a few days after the airlift ended, his former defense secretary, James Forrestal, committed suicide, leaping from a window in Bethesda Naval Hospital in Maryland. Forrestal left his post at Truman's request in March after he showed signs of a mental breakdown. The secretary's breakdown and death left Truman shaken and angry—he felt as though Forrestal's critics in the nation's press drove him to despair. Forrestal, however, had a history of depression and had not been a perfect fit within Truman's cabinet, clashing with the president over several proposed cuts in defense spending.

Truman chose Louis Johnson, a lawyer from Virginia who shared the president's enthusiasm for universal military training, as Forrestal's replacement. Johnson, a World War II veteran who helped found the American Legion, turned out to be a disaster. He alienated the brass and the rank and file in the Defense Department, cut the department's budget by more than $1 billion in 1949, and scrapped plans to build a huge new aircraft carrier, the USS *United States*. Although he continued in office until 1950, Johnson's imperious manner and cost-cutting style made him extremely unpopular with the nation's top military officers.

At the heart of the dispute over the USS *United States* was the armed services' plan for another major war. The Navy believed it needed a super-carrier in order for its airplanes to take part in air operations in the event of a nuclear or large conventional war. The Air Force jealously guarded its proprietary role over the nation's air defenses—in the event of nuclear war, its arsenal, and not the Navy's fliers, would provide the decisive role. The dispute seemed academic, but as the summer passed, Harry Truman once again found himself considering the prospects for war and a broader ideological conflict with Communism.

The nationalist Chinese were on the verge of collapse in the summer of 1949 as Mao Zedong's Communist army prepared for one final push in the southern region of the vast country. As Mao's victory became inevitable, Truman's critics, especially those in the Republican Party, blamed the White House for losing China to Communism. The pending perjury trial of Alger Hiss, the former State Department official accused of Communist sympathies, gave Truman's critics an opportunity to raise the specter of Communists operating within the government, manipulating policy to ensure Communist victories abroad. Truman sought to clear the record with the publication of a huge report containing State Department correspondence about China from 1944 to 1949. The report concluded that even though the United States had given the Chinese nationalists $2 billion in aid, Washington was unable to control events in China. The nationalists lacked strong leadership, the report said, and many in the movement were corrupt. The "China report" backfired on Truman as critics jumped on its findings to argue that the president and his policymakers bungled the war, paving the way for the imminent Communist victory. Ambitious Republicans in Congress, including Representative Richard Nixon of California and Senator Joseph McCarthy of Wisconsin, were eager to suggest that more than incompetence was involved—they saw, or said they saw, evidence of a Communist conspiracy at the highest levels of the Truman administration.

Matters became graver still on September 20, when Truman learned that the Soviets successfully tested a nuclear bomb, ending Washington's monopoly on humankind's most fearsome weapon. While U.S. intelligence had been picking up evidence that the Soviets were trying to build a nuclear weapon, word of the test nevertheless came as a profound shock. America's postwar sense of omnipotence was based on its possession of the bomb. America had it, and nobody else did. The bomb was the great equalizer in Washington's military strategy—the Soviets had a decided advantage in conventional weapons, but in the event of war, the United States had the most destructive weapon ever created. The Soviets risked annihilation if they moved against the West.

Now, however, all was changed, at home as well as abroad. The United States was no longer the world's lone superpower. That unpleasant reality would have ramifications for U.S. foreign relations as well as American domestic politics. Truman's critics would have a field day—first China, now a Soviet atom bomb.

The president was inclined to keep quiet about the Soviet test, but aides persuaded him that too many people knew about it. After all, dozens of airplanes over the Pacific detected extraordinary amounts of radioactivity in the air. Aides persuaded Truman that he ought to make a formal announcement to the American people, rather than react to the news when it leaked out, as it inevitably would. Press secretary Charlie Ross handed out a statement to the press on September 23. "We have evidence that within recent weeks an atomic explosion occurred in the USSR," the statement read.[2]

Truman asserted that the Soviet blast proved the need for "truly enforceable international control of atomic energy, which this government and the large majority of the members of the United Nations support."

Truman's citation of the United Nations and the opinions of its members spoke to his sincere belief that the fledgling organization would be able to bring order to the fast-developing chaos of the postwar era. For all of Truman's small-town parochialism and sometimes narrow approach to complex problems, he was a committed internationalist who believed in the ideals of the United Nations. The problems of war, disease, injustice, and development no longer respected boundaries. The United States learned during two world wars that oceans no longer served as a buffer against the world's problems. Likewise, Truman believed, individual nations could not resolve global problems.

Coincidentally, as the Cold War took an ominous turn in the late summer of 1949, Harry Truman traveled to New York to preside over the laying of the cornerstone for the new United Nations headquarters on the East Side of Manhattan. The international situation on the morning of October 24, 1949, could hardly have been grimmer: the world now had two nuclear powers with the capability of delivering unimaginable destruction, and one of those powers, the United States, was discussing the development of an even more destructive weapon, a hydrogen bomb. The Soviet explosion not only changed the power dynamics of the postwar order, but it also set in motion humankind's first nuclear arms race.

But it was peace, not war, on Harry Truman's mind as he stood on a temporary podium erected on Manhattan's Forty-second Street. To his right, traffic flowed in the distance along the Franklin D. Roosevelt Drive into a tunnel underneath the new UN site. Joining the president on the podium was New York governor Thomas E. Dewey, the man Truman defeated in 1948.

Truman's speech established both a moral and practical framework for the UN as it matured and took on a more forceful role in mediating the world's disputes and attempting to nurture justice and equality around the globe. "The United Nations," Truman said, "is essentially an expression of the moral nature of man's aspirations." The president, then, saw the UN not only as a practical response to the world's serial attempts at mass suicide, but as an affirmation of morality. Mankind aspired to peace, not conflict. "Because the United Nations is the dynamic expression of what all peoples of the world desire, because it sets up a standard of right and justice for all nations, it is greater than any of its members." The UN's mission and ideals, then, were greater and more urgent than the nations who joined it—including the United States. No president would have dared utter such an assertion before World War II.

Truman said that the UN's success would be "measured by the extent to which the rights of individual human beings are realized. And it will be measured by the extent of our economic and social progress." His use of the word "our" was striking, for he was not speaking of his fellow Americans, but of the citizens of the world. The progress he sought was global, not confined to a single nation-state.

Truman also praised the UN commitment to economic development, revisiting a theme he struck in his inaugural address. "Today, at least half of mankind lives in dire poverty. Hundreds of millions of men, women, and children lack adequate food, clothing, and shelter. We cannot achieve permanent peace and prosperity in the world until the standard of living in underdeveloped areas is raised."

Truman reaffirmed his support for the UN's Atomic Energy Commission, emphasizing his backing of greater international regulation of atomic energy, an issue given greater urgency a month earlier when the Soviets exploded their bomb. Effective international control of atomic energy, he said, would "make the prohibition of atomic weapons effective, and at the same time promote the peaceful development of atomic energy on a cooperative basis." Even as he spoke, some of his top nuclear aides were debating the feasibility, and the morality, of developing weapons vastly more powerful that the Soviet atomic bomb.

Truman concluded his speech with a visionary passage about the UN's commitment not to member nation-states, but to the individual citizens of the world. In the end, he said, the UN would seek to settle not national disputes, but "human problems."

"The challenge of the twentieth century is the challenge of human relations, and not of impersonal natural forces," he said. "The real dangers confronting us today have their origins in outmoded habits of thought, in the inertia of human nature, and in preoccupation with supposed national interest to the detriment of the common good.

"Our faith," he continued, "is in the betterment of human relations. Our vision is of a better world in which men and nations can live together, respecting one another's rights and cooperating in building a better life."

Harry Truman was the UN's most important ally during the late 1940s. His unwavering commitment to the institution and internationalism in general put an end, finally, to lingering American isolationism.

And, when the time came for the UN to make a stand for its ideals, it sided with Harry Truman during one of his presidency's gravest crises.

It was termed a "police action," but the war in Korea was difficult
and bloody. Here, the 1st U.S. cavalry prepares for battle.

CHAPTER 21

Korea

Address to the Nation
July 19, 1950

TRACK 21

THE NEW YEAR OF 1950 BROUGHT WITH IT CHANGES AND CHALLENGES reminiscent of the early days of Harry Truman's tenure. Two of his most trusted advisors—young Clark Clifford, whose political advice and speechwriting skills were invaluable, and New Deal holdover David Lilienthal, head of the government's atomic energy program—both made plans to leave Washington in February. Lilienthal had been in Washington since the early days of the Roosevelt administration, when he ran the Tennessee Valley Authority. Unlike so many of those early New Dealers, Lilienthal never thought of Harry Truman as some sort of usurper, an unworthy successor to the great Franklin Roosevelt. But Lilienthal was on the wrong side of a tremendous policy debate within the Truman Administration. He and his agency, the Atomic Energy Commission, vigorously opposed proposals to develop a new, more devastating weapon known as the hydrogen bomb. Military officials and Secretary of State Dean Acheson saw the H-bomb as a counter to the Soviets' development of an atomic bomb. But Lilienthal and others saw the bomb as an appalling and even immoral weapon that only increased the odds that human beings would wipe out each other and the planet. Truman decided in favor of the bomb, although that did not prompt Lilienthal's decision

198 ౿ GIVE 'EM HELL

to retire. It was, after nearly two decades in government service, simply time for him to go.

Clifford was a relative newcomer, having joined Truman's staff as a counsel in 1946. During the ensuing years, his keen political instincts, speechwriting skills, and growing collection of contacts served Truman well. The president trusted him on matters of politics (Clifford was a key figure in the president's reelection campaign), as well as policy (Clifford argued in favor of U.S. recognition of Israel, to the dismay of then-Secretary of State George Marshall).

The absence of Clifford and Lilienthal made the early months of 1950 that much more difficult for Truman. He faced a growing Republican insurgency over Communist gains in China and within America's own borders—if the charges of an obscure U.S. senator from Wisconsin were to be believed. In February, Senator Joseph R. McCarthy delivered a speech in West Virginia in which he asserted, without any proof, that he was aware of 205 known Communists who were working in the federal government, presumably passing along government secrets and otherwise betraying their country. McCarthy received some notice in the press, but at the time he seemed more of an annoyance than a threat, even though he attacked Secretary of State Acheson by name as a virtual Communist sympathizer. Truman tried to dismiss McCarthy's charges, saying that he believed the senator was "the greatest asset the Kremlin has."[1]

As the president adjusted to life without two key advisors and to a political culture that was far less civil and far more disturbing than ever before, his national security staff was working on a document designed to adjust American foreign policy to what it saw as dark new realities. The triumph of Communism in China, the Soviets' atomic bomb, and the specter of Communist aggression abroad and infiltration at home led to an intense reexamination of American foreign policy in a world in which ideological conflict was unavoidable and continuous. The National Security Council, established in 1947 in legislation that also created the Central Intelligence Agency and a new Department of Defense to replace the old War Department, produced a document known as NSC-68 in early April. It was one of the most momentous government reports of the postwar era. In language better suited to a sensational newspaper report, NCS-68 warned of a world in which the United States would be in constant peril from its

nuclear-armed antagonist, the Soviet Union. The Soviets had an astonishing advantage in conventional armed forces, with an army of more than 2.5
million men (compared to a U.S. Army of just over half a million), and they
were determined to use their advantage to spread Communism by force
throughout the world. While the United States enjoyed an advantage in
nuclear weapons, the fifty-eight-page document warned that the Soviets
would have the advantage within five years.

According to the document's primary author, Paul Nitze, the United
States had no choice but to contain the Communist threat. Doing so would
require a massive military buildup—after years in which Truman sought
to cut the Defense Department's budget. Nitze drew his argument in part
from those made by Soviet specialist George Kennan, a State Department
official who argued in 1946 that Soviet Communism and Western social
democracy were incompatible and destined to conflict with each other.
Kennan saw the Soviets as an aggressive threat to the United States,
internally and externally, arguing that Washington had to prepare for what
John F. Kennedy would later call a "twilight struggle" with Moscow. The
Soviets themselves, Kennan stated, were paranoid and therefore likely to
conduct the conflict not on traditional grounds of national interest, but on
an unstable, irrational basis that would make negotiations difficult if not
impossible. At stake, Kennan argued, was the very existence of the United
States and Western ideas of freedom and liberty. The Kennan argument
influenced the work of Clark Clifford and George Elsey, who wrote a huge
analysis of Soviet-American relations calling for American action to stop the
spread of Soviet-style Communism in late 1946.

The new document, NSC-68, amplified the arguments of Kennan,
Clifford, and Elsey, arguing that containment would not be possible with-
out "a more rapid build-up of political, economic, and military strength."[2]
Unofficial estimates, not included in the report, suggested a tripling of the
Defense Department's $15 billion budget.

Truman received the report in April but did little about its breathless
recommendations. He was as wary of Soviet intentions as anyone, but he
was also skeptical of efforts to bulk up defense spending, a mindset his
secretary of defense, Louis Johnson, shared.

That all changed on the night of June 24, 1950, when the Communist
government of North Korea sent tens of thousands of troops into South

Korea in an attempt to overthrow its pro-Western government and unite the peninsula under Communist rule. Truman received the news while relaxing in Missouri. He flew back to Washington the following day, fearful that the world, not just Korea, was about to descend into war again. If the North Koreans were not challenged, he thought, "no small nation would have the courage to resist threats and aggression by stronger Communist neighbors."[3] His generation of Americans had learned a lesson about unpunished aggression—it led to more aggression, followed by war and catastrophe.

The United Nations Security Council, facing the first grave crisis of its young existence, declared by a 9–0 vote that North Korea had committed a breach of peace—the Soviets were not able to block the vote because they were boycotting the Council to protest the continued membership of the defeated nationalist Chinese government, which withdrew to the island of Taiwan in 1949 after Mao's victory on the mainland. The Council called on North Korea to withdraw immediately.

The division of Korea, like the division of Germany, was a product of two wars—World War II and the Cold War. The peninsula was divided into two zones of occupation after the war—an American zone and a Soviet zone, divided arbitrarily at the 38th parallel. The division was meant to be temporary, but plans for an all-Korea national election were foiled in 1948 when the Soviets refused to cooperate. Instead, they installed a Communist government in their zone, while elections proceeded in the U.S. zone. Two rival governments were then established, divided by ideology and the 38th parallel.

The Truman administration was not overly concerned about the partition, for Korea seemed a highly unlikely flash point in Washington's Eurocentric vision of the Cold War. The Truman administration began withdrawing troops as the newly elected government of President Syngman Rhee established control in the south, now known as the Republic of Korea. By the spring of 1950, no U.S. soldiers were on Korean soil. The North Korean onslaught took Truman and his top advisors—not to mention the South Korean military—by complete surprise.

Truman assembled his top military and diplomatic aides for a long series of meetings in the days after the invasion. Nobody, least of all Truman, doubted that the United States had to act on behalf of its embattled allies in South Korea. Truman and his advisors believed that Moscow was behind the attack, yet another example of Soviet determination to prey on small, non-Communist countries on the borderlands between Communism and Western-style liberalism. Truman quickly authorized General Douglas MacArthur, the hero of the Pacific war who now oversaw the U.S. occupation of Japan, to resupply the South Korean government with weapons and ammunition. The United States, Truman decided, would provide further support from the air and from elements of the Seventh Fleet in the Pacific. He did not, however, issue orders to move ground troops to Korea. He still hoped to avoid engagement on the ground. "I don't want to go to war," he told his cabinet.[4]

He did, however, want to go to the United Nations, an institution he supported with words and actions since its founding. He saw the UN as a global bully pulpit, an institution that could bring the moral force of the world upon aggressors. His top diplomatic aides, led by Secretary of State Dean Acheson, lobbied UN members to rally behind South Korea. On June 27, the UN formally asked its members to join the United States in resisting North Korea's aggression.

As the world rallied to support South Korea, the nation rallied in support of Harry Truman. Republicans and Democrats alike approved of the president's swift and unambiguous support for South Korea. The party's candidate for president in 1936, Alfred Landon of Kansas, praised Truman's "raw courage."[5] But some of the praise was tempered by concerns in Congress that Truman was moving forward with plans for war without input—or authorization—from Congress. The Constitution, after all, empowered not the president but the national legislature—the voice of the people—with the power to declare war. The question then became whether the conflict was, in fact, a war. During a press conference, Truman agreed with a reporter's description of the conflict as a "police action," a phrase that critics would later seize as evidence that his war policy was half-hearted and not designed for victory.

South Korea seemed on the verge of defeat in late June. At MacArthur's request, Truman dispatched two divisions to South Korea on June 30, and further authorized air strikes over North Korea, although pilots were instructed to avoid areas near North Korea's borders with China and the Soviet Union. Even as the nation drifted to war, Truman chose measured responses as he sought to avoid the nightmare of another world war. He was concerned about Mao's response, and about Soviet intentions elsewhere in the world. "Must be careful not to cause a general Asiatic war," he wrote in his diary.[6] The Soviets sent word to Washington that they would not send troops to support the North Koreans, but Truman continued to calibrate his response in an effort to make sure the conflict remained confined to the Korean peninsula.

On July 7, the Security Council formally granted Truman's request to establish a coordinated UN force under the command of an American general. Truman chose General MacArthur to lead the multinational force, which would fight under the blue flag of the United Nations. About ten thousand U.S. troops were on the ground, joining some twenty-five thousand South Koreans against nearly a hundred thousand North Koreans who were pressing a relentless, well-planned offensive. American troops were ill-prepared, equipped with outdated weapons from World War II and utterly unfamiliar with the Korean terrain. They withdrew, stubbornly but consistently, in the face of the North's onslaught. Meanwhile, supplies and reinforcements from Britain, Australia, France, and other nations were funneling in through the southern port of Pusan, the largest city still in South Korea's hands. MacArthur was already planning a brilliant but risky counter-attack once his force had sufficient numbers and resources.

Truman had yet to consult Congress about the nation's new military commitment. Few voices, however, protested his unilateral decision-making. On July 19, the president sent a message to Capitol Hill asking Congress for $10 billion to rebuild and resupply the nation's armed services. New taxes, he said, and a larger army would be necessary for the nation's new, but undeclared, war.

That night, Truman addressed the country on radio and television. Although he had addressed the situation in Korea in news conferences and other public statements, he had not yet outlined his plans to the nation as a whole. Dressed in jacket and tie and doing his best to ignore the hot glare of primitive television lights, Truman began speaking at 10:30 p.m. Washington time.

Typically, he wasted little time getting to his point. North Korea's "act of raw aggression" showed that "the international Communist movement is willing to use armed force to conquer independent nations." The attack on South Korea was an attack on the security of all free nations, but equally significant, Truman described it as a "violation of the charter of the United Nations." The president intended to frame the conflict not as a mere skirmish in the Cold War, but as a direct violation of the UN's principles, justifying a response in defense of those principles. The UN's Security Council, he noted, "was set up to act in such cases as this—to stop outbreaks of aggression in a hurry before they develop into general conflicts." Truman emphasized the process by which the Security Council called on North Korea to withdraw and then asked members of the UN to join together to resist the aggressors. Truman's carefully crafted argument sought to isolate North Korea and to emphasize the collective nature of the UN response. "The free nations have now made it clear that lawless aggression will be met with force," Truman told the country. "The free nations have learned the fateful lesson of the 1930s. That lesson is that aggression must be met firmly. Appeasement leads only to further aggression and ultimately to war."

The lessons of the 1930s also taught that international organizations needed more than just words and resolutions to halt aggression. The League of Nations had been unable to stop the Italian invasion of Ethiopia and other prewar conflicts, condemning it to irrelevancy as wider conflicts loomed. Truman noted that several nations answered the UN's call with troops, airplanes, and other war material. A multinational force was assembling not under separate national flags, but under a unified UN command. "The prompt action of the United Nations to put down lawless aggression, and the prompt response to this action by free peoples all over the world, will stand as a landmark in mankind's long search for a rule of law among nations," Truman said.

While the war was contained to a small slice of soil on the great Asian land mass, Truman emphasized that victory would require sacrifices not unlike those imposed during World War II, a giant global enterprise that required tremendous resources. Truman told his fellow Americans that they would have to pay for a larger army, for new and better military equipment, for strengthened defenses at home. Young men would be subject to the draft; families would be required to pay more taxes to support the troops. He asked Congress for powers that would allow Washington "to guide the flow of materials into essential uses, to restrict their use for nonessential purposes, and to prevent the accumulation of unnecessary inventories."

These were total-war measures, adopted in the early 1940s when government took command of the economy for the war. Truman believed these steps were required again, painful though they were to a nation that loathed excessive government intervention.

And there would be other kinds of pain as well. It would be necessary, he said, "to make substantial increases in taxes. This is a contribution to our national security that every one of us should stand ready to make." And he warned against civilians who hoarded foods and other goods. "That is foolish—I say that is foolish, and it is selfish, very selfish, because hoarding results in entirely unnecessary local shortages," he said.

"We have the resources to meet our needs. Far more important, the American people are unified in their belief in democratic freedom. We are united in detesting Communist slavery," he said, fairly spitting out the final two words.

Not once did Truman use the word "war" to describe the conflict to which he was committing so much American power, prestige, resources, and troops. Within two months, U.S. casualties surpassed ten thousand. But there was light at the end of the tunnel—in late summer, Truman approved MacArthur's extremely risky plan to land thousands of UN troops behind enemy lines at Inchon, while other UN troops launched a counter-attack from their beachhead in Pusan in the south.

North Korea's seemingly unbeatable army was shattered and in retreat by late September. The war—the police action—seemed just about over.

President Truman and General Douglas MacArthur had very different
ideas about U.S. goals in Korea, and when MacArthur flouted
Truman's directions, he was dismissed.

CHAPTER 22

Conflict and Stalemate

Address to the Nation on General MacArthur's Removal
April 11, 1951

TRACK 22

H ARRY TRUMAN HAD NEVER MET DOUGLAS MACARTHUR. THEY WERE TWO very different men from very different backgrounds. Truman was a small-town politician who retained his down-to-earth style and folksy demeanor even after years as the most powerful man on earth. MacArthur was the son of a Civil War hero and Medal of Honor winner who was raised to follow in his father's footsteps. He graduated at the top of his class at the U.S. Military Academy in West Point, New York, and earned a reputation as a brilliant general during World War II and as a veritable American Caesar while presiding over the reconstruction of Japan's civilian government after the war. MacArthur was fond of dramatic, flowery phrases filled with sentiment and bravado, a far cry from Truman's straightforward, unadorned prose.

In the early fall of 1950, as troops under MacArthur's command seemed on the verge of victory, Harry Truman decided that it was time to meet the commander of UN forces. The president went more than halfway around the world to meet MacArthur—Truman flew nearly fifteen thousand miles to Wake Island in the Pacific to meet the General, whose journey from Tokyo covered just about four thousand miles.

The two men met on Sunday, October 15, and after some preliminary discussions, they and their aides convened a formal meeting in a small building on the tiny island. MacArthur told Truman that the conflict in Korea would be over by Thanksgiving, just about a month away. Troops, he said, would start returning home by Christmas.

Truman, to his own surprise, found the conversation pleasant—MacArthur was known to be imperious and difficult at times, but as he briefed the president, he exuded confidence without arrogance. The president was delighted with the general's assessment, but he expressed concern that either the Soviets or the Chinese might intervene on behalf of North Korea's disintegrating army. MacArthur seemed more concerned about the Soviets and their air power. The Chinese, he said, would be foolish to send ground forces to what would only be a mass slaughter. The Soviets, on the other hand, might be inclined to mount an air campaign, but he considered that unlikely.

Incredibly, given the distance Truman traveled to attend the meeting, the conference broke up after less than two hours. MacArthur said he was eager to get back to Tokyo to resume command of events in Korea, and Truman was happy to let him leave on a high note. When an aide suggested in a discreet note that the president ought to slow down the pace of talks with the general, Truman replied, "I want to get out of here before we get into trouble."[1]

There was trouble ahead, all right, but on Wake Island on that Sunday night, all was sweetness and light. Before MacArthur took his leave, Truman presented him with the nation's Distinguished Service Medal. Both men smiled for newspaper photographers and announced that the meeting had been a smashing success.

Two weeks later, on November 1, as MacArthur continued his mop-up operation beyond the 38th parallel in North Korea, two armed men tried to shoot their way into Blair House, where the Truman family lived during the renovation of the White House. It was an oppressively hot afternoon, and Truman was upstairs in his room, sprawled out on his bed wearing nothing but his underwear as he grabbed a few minutes rest before his next appointment. Shots rang out just before 2:30 p.m., startling the president, whose bedroom windows faced the street.

Two men dressed in suits opened fire on several police officers stationed outside Blair House. They planned to kill the officers, rush into the building, and murder the president in the name of Puerto Rican independence. The small security detail managed to foil the assassins, although one officer, Leslie Coffelt, was mortally wounded. One of the gunmen, Griselio Torresola, also died; the other, Oscar Collazo, was captured. (He was convicted of attempted murder and sentenced to death, but Truman commuted his sentence to life in prison. He was paroled nearly thirty years later.) Rumors swept Washington that the president had been shot, but Truman went on with his appointments that day. But he would never again walk from Blair House to his office in the White House, as he had done since renovations on the mansion began in 1948. A car outfitted with bulletproof windows took him to work from that day on.

In the days following Truman's close call, the president and his aides received disturbing news from Korea—confirmed reports of Chinese troops fighting in Korea on behalf of the North Koreans. MacArthur had told Truman on Wake Island that the war would be over by Thanksgiving and the troops would be home by Christmas. The general himself had labeled a planned new attack as an "end-the-war" offensive. The specter of Chinese troops reinforcing the North Koreans, however, worried Truman and his aides. This was precisely the scenario Truman discussed with MacArthur during their brief conference. The general, of course, said the Chinese would never cross the border, for such a move would be suicidal.

Thanksgiving came and went with no announced end of hostilities. The following day, November 24, as MacArthur launched what he believed would be the final attack of the war, more than a quarter million Chinese troops crossed into Korea, overwhelming the 8th U.S. Army. Stunned, MacArthur announced that "we face an entirely new war."[2]

Truman called an emergency meeting of his National Security Council on November 28 to discuss the nation's response to that new war. The news from Korea was all bad. United Nations forces were being pushed back and were taking heavy casualties. General Omar Bradley, chairman of the Joint Chiefs of Staff, had even more disturbing news. American intelligence reported the presence of three hundred enemy bombers in Manchuria, possibly preparing for missions in Korea. Among the options under discussion was a preemptive assault on the air fields in Manchuria, but that would widen the war beyond Korea's borders, with unknowable consequences. Secretary of State Dean Acheson warned that such an attack would certainly provoke a response from the Soviet Union. Acheson's predecessor at the State Department, George C. Marshall, was back in the cabinet as Truman's new secretary of defense. He argued against any unilateral American response, pointing out that the war was a United Nations effort, and it would serve neither the United States nor the UN to become involved in a wider war with China, although he conceded that many Americans would demand an aggressive American response to the Chinese intervention.

Truman and his aides decided that they would not widen the war, and that they would calibrate their actions to make sure that the Russians did not have a pretext for sending in troops of their own. But several days later, Truman blundered at a news conference when he said, amid reports of growing U.S. losses during a demoralizing retreat, that the United States would consider using an atomic bomb in Korea. The White House had to issue a quick clarification, saying that Truman had not authorized use of the weapon.

As the extent of the disaster in Korea became evident, with fresh reports of losses and continued retreat, MacArthur's strategy came under attack in the White House and in the nation's press. Some of the president's aides openly argued that MacArthur ought to be relieved of command. The nation's newspapers spoke of the inevitability of a new world war, although that was precisely what Truman was trying to avoid. Senator Joseph McCarthy of Wisconsin, plotting his way onto the national stage, argued that Truman ought to be impeached.

In the midst of these disasters, Charlie Ross, the president's friend and press secretary, died suddenly at the age of sixty-five. That night, December 5, the president attended a concert in Washington's Constitution Hall, where his daughter Margaret, a fledgling singer, performed music by some of Truman's favorite classical composers, including Mozart. The following morning, a critic for the *Washington Post*, Paul Hume, published a devastating critique of Miss Truman's performance. After praising her appearance and acknowledging that she had a nice voice, Hume wrote that "Miss Truman cannot sing very well." When Truman read the review, he took up a pen and wrote a hasty note to Hume, saying that he looked forward to meeting him. "When that happens," he wrote, "you'll need a new nose, a lot of beefsteak for black eyes, and perhaps a supporter below."[3] Hume published what was intended as a private note, so the nation and the world learned that the president of the United States threatened a journalist with physical harm. It was not Truman's finest hour, but as his daughter noted many years later, Hume's review came at a difficult time for the president. "His best friend had just died, the world situation was going from bad to awful, and now a critic was attacking his daughter with what seemed to be more malice than judgment," she wrote.[4] Truman later insisted that he reacted as any father would have—and that was the point. "It was Harry S. Truman, the human being, who wrote that note," he said afterwards.[5]

Coincidentally, the news began to change from awful to encouraging in late December, when a new ground commander, General Matthew Ridgway, took charge of the beaten, demoralized 8th U.S. Army. While the army continued its retreat south, leaving the South Korean capital, Seoul, to the enemy, Ridgway's leadership persuaded the troops that one day soon, they would turn and fight and win. But MacArthur was not so sanguine. He believed the United Nations troops were on the verge of a catastrophic, humiliating defeat, one that could be avoided if the Truman administration dropped atomic bombs by the dozens—perhaps as many as fifty—on Chinese cities and other targets. Although Truman himself had held out the possibility of using the atomic bomb weeks earlier, he almost immediately backtracked, and he certainly never took MacArthur's proposal seriously.

The 8th Army was back on the offensive in late January, around the same time that Truman declared a national emergency at home, allowing him to impose federal controls over prices and wages, just as Roosevelt did during World War II. Ridgway's performance on the field offered Washington a contrast with MacArthur's wild schemes to widen the war by attacking China. In late winter, with Ridgway's army winning back large chunks of South Korean territory, Truman was prepared to begin ceasefire talks through the United Nations. MacArthur was furious. He wanted not a return to the status quo—two Koreas, divided by the 38th parallel—but a conquest of the entire peninsula and the liberation of China from Communist rule. Before Truman could act on a ceasefire proposal, MacArthur issued a bellicose statement of his own, threatening China's cities and coastal ports with attacks that would endanger the government's very existence.

Truman was furious. MacArthur's statement, he wrote, "was in open defiance of my orders as President and as Commander in Chief. This was a challenge to the authority of the President under the Constitution." Truman decided that he had no choice. "I could no longer tolerate his insubordination."[6]

But he did, at least for a few days as he considered his course of action. Then, in early April, the former Republican Speaker of the House, Joseph Martin, revealed the contents of a letter MacArthur wrote to him after Martin complained that the White House refused to allow nationalist Chinese troops from Taiwan to augment the UN effort—a strategy that would have further inflamed the Communist Chinese. Martin said that if Truman didn't wish to win the war, he and his aides should be charged with murder of American soldiers. In his reply, MacArthur agreed with Martin's sentiments, saying that a Communist victory in Asia would lead to the collapse of Europe. He concluded with the now famous line, "There is no substitute for victory."[7]

A day later, on April 6, Truman convened his top aides to discuss MacArthur's letter. The military men—Marshall and Bradley—were not eager to call for MacArthur's head. The president, however, had his mind made up. "Rank insubordination," he wrote of MacArthur in his diary on the night of April 6. "I've come to the conclusion that our Big General in the Far East must be recalled."[8]

By April 10, his advisors all agreed: MacArthur had to go. That afternoon, Truman signed an order relieving MacArthur of his command. The decision was kept secret so that MacArthur wouldn't suffer the indignity of learning about his dismissal from a reporter. But after a newsman from the *Chicago Tribune* called the White House that night, asking about reports of a high-profile resignation in the Far East command, Truman and his aides called a postmidnight news conference to announce the president's decision. Truman was determined to set the agenda—he would not allow MacArthur to quit on his own. The White House press office distributed copies of Truman's order to sleepy reporters at 1:00 a.m. on the morning of April 11. The White House issued a written statement from Truman. "With deep regret," it read, "I have concluded that General of the Army Douglas MacArthur is unable to give his whole-hearted support to the policies of the United States Government and of the United Nations in matters pertaining to his duty…I have, therefore, relieved General MacArthur of his commands and have designated Lieutenant General Matthew B. Ridgway as his successor."[9]

Political figures and ordinary citizens woke up to learn that Harry Truman had fired one of the nation's great war heroes. The uproar was instantaneous and deafening. Republicans called for Truman's impeachment—one insisted that MacArthur's dismissal was proof that Communists were in charge of the country. Most of the nation's newspapers, however, supported Truman and the principle of civilian leadership of the military.

At ten thirty on the night of April 11, Harry Truman spoke to the nation via radio to explain not so much his decision, but his policy and goals in Korea. He did not refer to the day's top headline—MacArthur's dismissal—until he was well into the speech.

"In the simplest terms," he said, "what we are doing in Korea is this: we are trying to prevent a third world war." MacArthur, he would argue by implication, was not so eager to avoid a wider war, and so he had to be dismissed.

But before he mentioned the general by name, he defended his actions in a war that was growing increasingly unpopular at home. "If history has taught us anything," he said, "it is that aggression anywhere in the world is a threat to peace everywhere in the world." That message, he hoped, would resonate with an audience only six years removed from the end of World War II, a conflict born of unchallenged aggression in Europe and Asia. The war in Korea, he said, was the "boldest and most dangerous move the Communists have yet made." It was, Truman insisted, "part of a greater plan for conquering all of Asia."

Truman framed the conflict as part of a larger conflict with Communist aggression directed from Moscow. The United States had managed to contain the conflict to the Korean peninsula, and by doing so, "we have prevented aggression from succeeding and bringing on a general war." But he knew some of his listeners might wonder why he had not bombed enemy airfields in Manchuria and China, why he had not agreed to join forces with the nationalist Chinese on Taiwan. To do so, he said, would widen the war, and that was exactly what the Soviets wanted. "If we were to do these things, we would become entangled in a vast conflict on the continent of Asia and our task would become immeasurably more difficult all over the world. What would suit the ambitions of the Kremlin better than for our military forces to be committed to a full-scale war with Red China?"

Having made the case against all-out war, he explained why he decided to remove the popular MacArthur from command. The general, he said, did not agree with the administration's policy, one that sought "to make sure that the precious lives of our fighting men are not wasted."

Removing MacArthur, he said, would also remove "doubt or confusion as to the real purpose and aim of our policy."

"It was with the deepest regret that I found myself compelled to take this action," he said. "General MacArthur is one of our greatest military commanders. But the cause of world peace is much more important than any one individual."

That was it—in a speech of more than fifteen minutes, he devoted no more than three to General MacArthur. His broader aim was to counter the arguments which the general's supporters surely would make when the old soldier returned home to a hero's welcome. The war in Korea, Truman insisted, could not become another world war.

It did not. But it continued to drag on, taxing the public's patience and wearing down the president and his aides.

George C. Marshall served as Harry Truman's secretary of state
and secretary of defense. He was the man Truman most admired
in his cabinet.

Seizing the Mills

Address to the Nation on the Steel Crisis
April 8, 1952

TRACK 23

DOUGLAS MacARTHUR RETURNED HOME A HERO. HE WAS INVITED TO SPEAK before a joint session of Congress, where he used his smooth baritone and ornate phrases to good effect, finishing with words that would forever be associated with him. "Old soldiers never die," he said. "They just fade away." He promised that he, too, would fade away, like the proverbial old soldier that he was. But he did not. An election year approached, and Harry Truman's critics saw MacArthur as a potential candidate for the presidency in 1952. The prospect of MacArthur challenging the man who fired him delighted reporters, who fueled speculation of a titanic MacArthur-Truman presidential campaign. The White House was inundated with messages denouncing the president. "Quite an explosion," Truman wrote in his diary. "Was expected but I had to act. Telegrams and letters of abuse by the dozens."[1]

Truman was eligible to run again in 1952 because he was specifically exempted from the 22nd amendment, which not only limits presidents to two terms, but also bars those who succeed to the presidency from running more than once if they serve more than two years of their predecessor's term. Many Democrats assumed that Truman would run again, perhaps against MacArthur.

Through the fall of 1951, however, as the war in Korea settled into a stalemate and casualties continued to grow, Truman's popularity plunged and prospects for a Republican victory in 1952 grew brighter. The opposition sharpened its rhetoric accordingly. In June 1951, two months after MacArthur was fired, Republican senator Joseph McCarthy of Wisconsin delivered a long speech on the Senate floor during which he described George Marshall, Truman's secretary of defense, and Dean Acheson, the secretary of state, as active agents of an immense Communist conspiracy at home and abroad. The president was furious, but upon the advice of his cabinet and Democratic senators, he refused to respond to McCarthy's wild slanders, concluding that a roll in the mud with the senator from Wisconsin would diminish the office and dignity of the presidency.

Truman's silence only seemed to embolden McCarthy, for as months passed and interest in the '52 presidential campaign grew, McCarthy continued to accuse the administration of complicity in Communist conspiracies. Marshall, disgusted that a lifetime of service to his country had come to this, resigned in September, depriving Truman once again of the man he admired most in his cabinet.

Republicans like Robert Taft and others were eager to begin the new presidential campaign, convinced that this time, they really had Truman where they wanted him. Not only had the president alienated millions of voters by firing MacArthur, but summer and fall brought reports of corruption and wrongdoing in Truman's Internal Revenue Service, leading to resignations of top administrators. Truman's approval rating sank to just over 20 percent, a catastrophic figure on the eve of an election campaign.

Harry Truman seemed about to embark on yet another hopeless campaign. The press was filled with speculation about would-be successors from both parties. Among them was another general, Dwight Eisenhower, a man Truman respected and liked. Eisenhower was serving as commander in chief of NATO troops at Truman's request, and while he had not said anything about his political ambitions, the press was convinced that Ike would enter the campaign, although it was uncertain whether he would run as a Democrat or a Republican.

Truman wrote a personal note to Eisenhower on December 18, 1951, asking him what his intentions were. He implied that if Ike were to run, he would go home "and maybe run for the Senate." But if Eisenhower decided "to finish the European job," Truman suggested that he would run for another term to "keep the isolationists out of the White House," although in other correspondence and conversations, he suggested that he had no intention of running for reelection.

"I wish you would let me know what you intend to do," he asked Ike. "It will be between us and no one else."[2]

Eisenhower replied two weeks later, saying that he very likely would not run for president. But he clearly had a change of heart: he announced his candidacy for the Republican presidential nomination in early January 1952.

With his poll ratings sagging and Republicans gathering around the popular war hero, Truman considered his own future and his party's. He conferred with Governor Adlai Stevenson in late January, urging him to enter the race and assuring the governor of his support. One Democrat was already campaigning to take Truman's place—Kentucky Senator Estes Kefauver, who campaigned as a good-government alternative to the Truman White House. To the astonishment of the press and the White House, Kefauver defeated Truman in the New Hampshire primary. While the president didn't campaign in the state—indeed, he had not announced his intentions for 1952—Kefauver's victory was significant, for it signaled broad dissatisfaction with the president and the status quo.

"I have known what I am going to do since April 1950," Truman wrote in his diary in early February.[3] He shared his secret with the rest of the country on March 29, during an appearance at a Jefferson-Jackson Day dinner in Washington, D.C. Looking tan and relaxed after a short trip to his favorite hideaway, Key West, he stepped to the podium at 10:30 p.m. As a national radio audience tuned in, Truman reprised the achievements of the New Deal and Fair Deal, laid into Republican opponents of his politics and those of Franklin Roosevelt, and then, at last, made his intentions clear. "I shall not be a candidate for reelection," he said at the conclusion of his speech. "I have served my country long, and I think efficiently and honestly. I shall not accept a nomination."[4]

Truman decided that Adlai Stevenson was the best man to carry on a broad, internationalist foreign policy while continuing to expand on the legacies of the New Deal and Fair Deal. Stevenson, however, seemed a good deal less certain about his ambitions and abilities, to Truman's frustration.

The fight for the Democratic presidential nomination would go on to Chicago and the party's convention.

Presidential politics gave way to domestic realities within days of Truman's withdrawal from the campaign.

The nation's well-organized steelworkers had been working for three months without a contract while their union, the United Steel Workers, tried to negotiate a raise, their first in nearly two years. Truman's Wage Stabilization Board, a wartime measure that regulated increases in prices and wages, became involved in the talks, and after hearing the union's case for a pay increase, it recommended that the steelworkers get an additional 26 cents an hour, about a dime less than what the union demanded. Nevertheless, the steel workers accepted the board's decision. Management did not. The big steel companies, representing a critical sector of the manufacturing economy, argued that they could afford such an increase only if the government allowed them to hike prices by $12 a ton, even for lower-grade steel that was relatively cheaper to produce. Truman, prairie populist that he was, had little sympathy for big business. After all, as chair of a Senate investigating committee during World War II, he had examined war profiteering by big business at a time when the civilian population was being asked to save and sacrifice. Truman thought a price increase of about $4.50 would be fair. But management's demand for a $12 increase struck him as excessive and greedy, especially during a time of war. "The profits of the steel companies were constantly rising," he wrote. "The nation was drafting its men to serve on the field of battle, and I thought that the ammunition and arms manufacturers and their raw-material producers ought not to use the emergency to insist on extra profits," he wrote.[5]

The emergency to which Truman referred was, of course, the bloody stalemate in Korea. A shutdown of the steel industry, he feared, would deny U.S. troops the weapons and ammunition they needed to fight a capable and stubborn enemy in Asia.

The steel workers' union set a deadline of April 9 to reach an agreement. Otherwise, its 650,000 members would walk off the job, bringing production to a halt. Ironically, Truman had it in his power to postpone a strike by fiat, thanks to the Taft-Hartley Act that he opposed so strongly and vetoed, to no avail, in 1947. The law included a provision allowing the president to keep workers on their jobs for eighty days while federal officials studied any impasse with management. But Truman, instinctively sympathetic to the workers, rejected a postponement, arguing that the workers themselves had voluntarily postponed their strike for more than three months in vain hopes of reaching a settlement.

With the clock ticking, Truman consulted domestic policy advisors and even Fred Vinson, chief justice of the Supreme Court, about his options, including a federal seizure of the steel mills. Vinson and other legal scholars assured him that a federal takeover would be constitutional as an emergency measure taken in the interest of national security.

Truman made up his mind. With the steel workers making plans to man picket lines, Truman issued an executive order on April 8 declaring the government would take control of the nation's steel mills beginning at midnight. Ninety minutes before Washington got into the steel business, Truman spoke to the nation from the White House, explaining why he believed the federal government had both a right and a duty to seize privately held property and operate it in the public's interest.

Tersely, he told the nation that it faced a "grave danger." Steel, he said, was the nation's key industry, especially when troops were in the field. "If steel production stops, we will have to stop making the shells and bombs that are going directly to our soldiers at the front in Korea," he said. "If steel production stops, we will have to cut down and delay the atomic energy program. If steel production stops, it won't be long before we have to stop making engines for the Air Force planes."

As president, Truman had to think about "our soldiers in Korea" who were battling "the Chinese Communists," and "our soldiers and allies in Europe" who were "confronted by the military power massed behind the Iron Curtain." Steel production was the key to national defense. And so, he argued, steel was no ordinary industry, and a dispute between steelworkers and management was no ordinary labor problem.

"Therefore," he said, "I am taking two actions tonight. First, I am directing the secretary of commerce to take possession of the steel mills and to keep them operating." In addition, he said, he would call on management and labor to come to Washington to resolve their differences.

While the administration might play the role of mediator and facilitator in talks between the two warring parties in the steel dispute, Truman made it clear that he had his own ideas about who was right and who was wrong. The president had more than his share of problems with organized labor during his first term, and no high-powered company president could match the president's impatience with labor leaders like John L. Lewis of the United Mine Workers. Still, Truman instinctively sided with workers over management and capital, as he made clear in his speech to the nation.

Special federal regulations designed to stabilize wage and price increases, he said, had been applied to the unions and to management. "The union has accepted these rules," he said. "The companies have not accepted them. The companies insist that they must have price increases that are out of line with the stabilization rules…The companies have said, in short, that unless they can have what they want, the steel industry will shut down. That is the plain, unvarnished fact of the matter."

Truman laid the blame squarely on the shoulders of companies like the giant United States Steel and its competitors. "To hear the steel companies talk, you would think the wage increase recommended by the [federal Wage Stabilization] Board would wipe out their profits altogether," he said. In fact, he insisted, the "steel industry has never been so profitable as it is today." He rejected management's contention that it could not afford a wage increase of 26 cents an hour without a price increase of $12 a ton, an increase, he said, which would give them a profit of $26 or $27 a ton. "That's about the most outrageous thing I ever heard of," said Truman. He argued that if steel were allowed such price increases, other industries would demand similar consideration, setting off an inflationary spiral that would endanger prosperity and national security.

"The plain fact of the matter is that the steel companies are recklessly forcing a shutdown of the steel mills," Truman said. "They are trying to get special, preferred treatment, not available to any other industry. And they are apparently willing to stop steel production to get it."

He would not allow that to happen. Within an hour of the speech's conclusion, management of the nation's steel industry passed from private hands to the federal government. The mills kept working as outraged executives began a legal case against the president's actions. On June 2, the Supreme Court ruled in a 6–3 decision that Truman's actions were unconstitutional. Some in the majority, especially William O. Douglas, accepted Truman's good intentions, but argued that the seizure would set a dangerous precedent. (Chief Justice Vinson sided with the minority in support of Truman's actions.)

With Washington out of the steel business, the workers immediately went on strike, remaining off the job for seven weeks. Truman, bitter over the Court's decision, described the dispute as "U.S. Steel...against the little fellows."[6]

The mills were idle until late July, when Truman demanded that union and management come to Washington and figure out a settlement. They did. The workers received a raise of 21 cents an hour, and the companies raised prices by $5.20 a ton, a far cry from their original demand for a $12 increase.

Days after the settlement, Democrats gathered in Chicago chose Adlai Stevenson to be their candidate in the 1952 general election. Truman vowed to do everything in his power to ensure another Democratic presidential victory.

When Truman decided not to run for president again in 1952, he backed
Illinois governor Adlai Stevenson for the Democratic nomination.
Stevenson, however, lacked Truman's spirit on the campaign
trail and lost to Dwight Eisenhower.

CHAPTER 24

Defending the Constitution

Address at the National Archives
December 15, 1952

TRACK 24

Harry Truman was always a history buff. His reading of American history was immense; so, too, was his respect for the institutions set up during the nation's founding and passed on to him for safekeeping during a volatile and dangerous era.

As he neared the end of his tenure in the White House, Harry Truman had time to reflect on history—his own and the nation's. There was little question that a memorable period was coming to an end, for on election day in November, America's voters overwhelmingly chose a Republican, Dwight Eisenhower, as president, ending a twenty-year Democratic monopoly of the nation's highest office. Adlai Stevenson, Truman's designated heir, failed to stir the nation's passions as Truman had done in 1948. The governor of Illinois shared the outgoing president's broad policy views and philosophy, but had little of the spark and fighting spirit that so characterized Truman's legendary come-from-behind campaign in 1948. A nation looking for change found little reason to stick with what seemed like the status quo. Instead, voters gravitated to Eisenhower, a man with a wonderful record of service, a bright smile, and an amiable public disposition.

Truman was bitterly disappointed, not so much because he interpreted Stevenson's defeat as a personal repudiation, but because he had grown to dislike Eisenhower in a visceral, personal way. Eisenhower, Truman believed, should have defended the honor and patriotism of George C. Marshall when Republicans, including Joseph McCarthy, attacked the former general and two-time cabinet secretary as a dupe of an immense Communist conspiracy. While Eisenhower himself did not impugn Marshall's integrity, he said nothing when other Republicans did. What's more, he decided against delivering a planned speech defending Marshall's honor in McCarthy's home state of Wisconsin. He spoke instead of the Communist threat and the ways in which unnamed government officials in Washington had helped orchestrate the fall of China and the triumph of Communism in Eastern Europe. McCarthy was in the audience, delighted. He had heard that Eisenhower planned to defend Marshall and rushed to Wisconsin from Illinois to demand that the tribute be cut. It was. And that, Truman believed, was a sign of moral cowardice.

In the campaign's final weeks, Truman publicly lashed into Eisenhower for the first time. "He ought to despise McCarthy, just as I expected him to, and just as I do," he told a crowd in New York. "Now, in his bid for votes, he has endorsed Joe McCarthy for reelection..."[1] Privately, he was just as furious. In a letter to a cousin in Missouri, Nellie Noland, Truman complained that Eisenhower had "taken up with" McCarthy and had "completely distorted the truth on Korea."[2]

Eisenhower, however, was not the only presidential candidate who incurred Truman's wrath that fall. His own standard-bearer, Stevenson, blundered into what seemed to be an explicit criticism of the president's years in office. Asked what he would do to clean up the "mess" in Washington—a favorite theme of Republicans in 1952—Stevenson separated himself from Truman, saying that he had won the nomination and was campaigning on his own, that his campaign headquarters was in Illinois rather than in Washington, and that he had removed traditional politicians from the leadership of the Democratic Party. Truman could hardly contain his anger. In a letter addressed to "my dear Governor," Truman wrote that "the presidential nominee and his running mate are trying to beat the Democratic President instead of the Republicans and the General of the Army who heads the ticket...You fired and balled up the Democratic Committee Organization that I've been creating over the last four years. I'm telling you to take your crackpots, your high socialites with their noses in the air, run your campaign and win if you can…Best of luck to you from a bystander who has become disinterested."[3] Wisely, Truman vented and then decided against sending the letter. He kept it, though, and filed it in his personal papers.

The weeks after Eisenhower's election were busy as Truman tried to arrange for a smooth transition of power—the first since Herbert Hoover gave way to Franklin Roosevelt in the winter of 1932–33. Eisenhower called on the president on November 18 for what was a chilly policy meeting between two men whose former affection for each other was now a distant memory. Less than a week later, on November 28, Truman rose before dawn to write in his diary. The White House, he noted, was quiet, so much so that he could hear airplanes warming up and the slight roar of early morning traffic. In a bedroom near his, Madge Wallace, his mother-in-law, was nearing her death at the age of ninety, attended to by a battery of doctors and nurses as she slipped into a coma. Truman hoped she would live to see Christmas in the White House. She did not—she died a few days later, on December 5, in the White House.

The building itself was finally open again after the massive renovations begun in 1948. The Trumans moved back into the mansion from Blair House in late March, just before the president made it clear that he would not seek another four-year lease on the place. And what a place it was—the renovation added more than forty rooms, including a television studio and a massive bomb shelter designed to serve as a headquarters during a nuclear attack. As Truman continued to write in his diary in the early hours of November 28, he reflected on the terms and careers of the men and women who lived in the great house before him. "This old house is a most remarkable one," he wrote. Jefferson greeted diplomats there "in house slippers and a dressing gown." James Monroe imported French furniture to decorate the house and soon was "catching hell" from critics who thought the president of the United States should buy American. On and on he went for several paragraphs, speaking of long-dead presidents as if he knew them—as he felt he did. Truman would later say that only a person who has been president can understand the burdens of that office. As Truman prepared to pass on those burdens to Eisenhower, his thoughts turned to "old Andy Jackson and his rough, tough backwoodsmen walking on the (White House) furniture" and John Tyler, who "had his problems with Congress." Tyler, he slyly noted, "succeeded in annexing Texas. Now whether that accomplishment was an asset or not I'm unable to say."[4] The Lone Star state broke ranks with the solidly Democratic South weeks earlier, supporting Eisenhower over Stevenson.

History, he decided, would be kinder to him than the press was. After his mother-in-law died, he anticipated that critics would attack him for using his presidential plane to fly his family and his mother-in-law's body back to Missouri—some had criticized his use of the airplane, nicknamed Independence (the moniker of Air Force One was not yet in use), when he flew home for his mother's funeral in 1947. "To hell with them," he wrote of his critics. "When history is written they will be the sons of bitches, not I."[5]

Harry Truman's sense of history and his reverence for the nation's founding documents and principles served him well in one of his final speeches as president. On December 15, 1952, Truman spoke at the National Archives in downtown Washington, just a few minutes from the White House, where he commemorated the opening of a new display area for the Declaration of Independence, the Constitution, and the Bill of Rights. As official Washington was engaged in transition, Harry Truman emphasized the unchanging principles of American government, principles that applied to both major political parties and to all officials who swore to uphold the nation's ideals and laws. The ceremony, he noted, took place on a day designated as "Bill of Rights Day" throughout the country, for it was on December 15, 1791, that the first ten amendments to the Constitution were ratified. Truman used the ceremony and the anniversary to explain why the documents to be enshrined in a new exhibit hall remained important, nearly two centuries after they were written.

"In many countries men swear to be loyal to their king, or to their nation," he said. "Here we promise to uphold and defend a great document. This is because the document sets forth our idea of government. And beyond this, with the Declaration of Independence, it expresses our idea of man. We believe that man should be free. And these documents establish a system under which man can be free and set up a framework to protect and expand that freedom."

In the context of late 1952, with American soldiers fighting in Korea and the world divided by a Cold War between West and East, Truman could hardly avoid current events even as he celebrated ideals put down on paper in the late eighteenth century. The specter of Communism haunted many of his speeches. This one, even though mostly ceremonial, was no exception.

Freedom and liberty, the ideals enshrined in the documents he celebrated, were under siege around the world, he said. "We are uniting the strength of free men against this threat," he said of Communism. "We are resisting Communist aggression and will continue to resist the Communist threat with all our will and with all our strength."

While such rhetoric might have been expected given the tensions between West and East, Truman added a sharp rejoinder aimed at those who despised Communism as much as he did, but who also seemed to regard the nation's founding laws and ideals to be an obstacle rather than a bulwark in fighting the Cold War. He did not mention Senator McCarthy and his allies, although the reference was clear.

The idea of freedom, he said, "is in danger from others as well as the Communists. There are some who hate Communism but who, at the same time, are unwilling to acknowledge the ideals of the Constitution as the supreme law of the land. They are the people who believe it is too dangerous to proclaim liberty throughout all the land to all its inhabitants. What these people really believe is that the Preamble (of the Constitution) ought to be changed from 'We, the people,' to read, 'Some of us—some of the people of the United States, but not including those we disapprove of or disagree with.'"

Those unnamed Americans—everybody in the audience, including Chief Justice Fred Vinson and top administrators of the Archives, could identify Truman's targets—were "enclosing the spirit as well as the letter of the original Constitution in a glass case, sealed off from the living nation.

"All freedom-loving nations, not the United States alone, are facing a stern challenge from the Communist tyranny. In the circumstances, alarm is justified…But alarm is one thing, and hysteria is another. Hysteria impels people to destroy the very thing they are struggling to preserve. Invasion and conquest by Communist armies would be a horror beyond our capacity to imagine. But invasion and conquest by Communist ideas of right and wrong would be just as bad. For us to embrace the methods and morals of Communism in order to defeat Communist aggression would be a moral disaster worse than any physical catastrophe. If that should come to pass, then the Constitution and the Declaration would be utterly dead."

In equating the methods of McCarthy and his followers with those of Communist aggressors, Harry Truman made it clear that he believed the nation's founding principles were in danger from within as well as from without. In the waning days of 1952, few would echo his brave and challenging words. But in the end, as was so often the case, he was proven correct.

Once his long years of service in Washington were over,
Harry Truman returned home to Independence.

CHAPTER 25

Mr. Citizen

Farewell Address to the Nation
January 15, 1953

TRACK 25

ARRY TRUMAN WAS A HAPPY MAN AS THE END OF HIS TERM NEARED. HE enjoyed being president as much as any of his predecessors, and probably more than most. But he also looked forward to returning home to Missouri and resuming life as a citizen—the highest rank, he pointed out, in a democratic republic. Elected officials, including the president, were but servants of the people, Harry Truman often noted. So the transition from president to citizen was, in fact, a promotion.

Years of honorable public service were a joy, but they were not without burdens. "No one knows what responsibility the presidency puts on a man," Truman wrote in a letter to his cousin, Ethel Noland, on January 2, 1953. "He is the chief executive, the commander in chief of all the armed forces, the top man in his party, the social head of the state, and the president of the United States." None of the great figures in history— Alexander the Great, Caesar, Napoleon—"had the power or the world influence" of the president.[1]

For his part, Harry Truman intended to follow the example of the great Roman general Cincinnatus, who was called into service to defend the Roman republic and then, his duty done and victory won, returned to his farm and the life of a Roman citizen. The example of Cincinnatus had inspired George Washington, as Truman knew, and now he intended to follow the example of both men. At the age of sixty-eight, healthy and fit, he intended to travel with Bess and otherwise enjoy living without the burdens of the presidency.

White House staff observed that Truman was noticeably happy and relaxed as his tenure neared its end. The country, however, was not quite so jolly. Truman's approval rating was very low—polls showed that only about a third of Americans had a favorable opinion of his job performance. The war in Korea was highly unpopular, and that war was Harry Truman's war. Otherwise, however, the country had every reason to wish their departing president well, for he had presided over a period of extraordinary economic growth. Labor unrest was tamed, unemployment was negligible, wages were up without sparking inflation, and millions of soldiers had been reintegrated into the nation's work force. Overseas, despite the ongoing conflict in Korea and tensions with the Soviet Union, America enjoyed unprecedented influence and prestige. The Marshall Plan rebuilt Western Europe. American air power saved West Berlin from starvation and surrender. The American occupation of Japan transformed that nation into a modern democracy. And the United States was committed to the ideals of collective security embodied in the United Nations organization.

Harry Truman rarely doubted that historians would be kinder to him than the public was during his final weeks in office. That confidence, together with his eager anticipation of civilian life, brought a sense of joy and accomplishment to the White House even as the president, his family, and longtime staffers prepared to go their separate ways. Winston Churchill dropped by in early January for a farewell visit with the president and his cabinet. After a rollicking dinner, which included a discussion of the president's skills as a piano player, Churchill took the president aside and confessed that he had been worried about Truman's abilities when Franklin Roosevelt died in 1945. "I misjudged you badly," Churchill told Truman. "Since that time, you, more than any other man, have saved Western civilization."[2] Such an endorsement surely would pick up anybody's spirits, not that Truman needed any such confidence builders, even in the face of public disapproval.

Harry Truman delivered one final speech as president, on the night of January 15, 1953. He spoke from the Oval Office, a place, he reminded

Americans, where great decisions had been made during the previous eight years. Truman's farewell was a masterpiece of plain speaking, the style that suited him best. In his own way, with his own words, he spoke to millions in the way Franklin Roosevelt did so many years earlier—as one human being speaking to another human being. So often in more formal circumstances, Truman's delivery sounded forced and stiff, but not on this night. He spoke in the straightforward, declarative sentences that served him well behind the scenes, when he used the powers of the presidency to persuade politicians, heads of government, and union leaders to do what he thought best.

At 10:30 at night, Harry Truman began his goodbyes to the nation he led for nearly eight years. "In speaking to you tonight," he said firmly and plainly, "I have no new revelations to make—no political statements, no policy pronouncement. There are simply a few things in my head that I want to say to you. I want to say 'good-bye' and 'thanks for the help.'"

But, of course, he wanted to say a bit more than that. Just as he reflected privately on his tenure as president, he wished to reminisce in public about the crises, decisions, and events of his presidency. He was in an expansive, upbeat mood, recalling the many trips he made overseas, the shock he and the nation shared when Franklin Roosevelt died, the challenges the nation met immediately after the end of World War II and the almost immediate beginning of the Cold War. But these memories were no mere exercise in nostalgia—he had a point to make, and he spoke to it directly just as he spoke to his listeners directly.

"I want all of you to realize how big a job, how hard a job, [the presidency] is," he said. "Not for my sake, because I am stepping out of it, but for the sake of my successor...Regardless of your politics, whether you are Republican or Democrat, your fate is tied up with what is done here in this room. The president is the president of the whole country. We must give him our support as citizens of the United States. He will have mine, and I want you to give him yours."

While that grace note is a routine part of American political discourse—an outgoing president often asks the country to support a successor regardless of party—Truman worked behind the scenes to make the transition to Eisenhower as smooth as possible, despite the frosty relations between the two men. Truman conceded that historians would one day note that the world entered the atomic age and the Cold War started during his tenure in office. But he argued that the decisions he made would lead to victory over Communism, a victory which he insisted would not require the use of nuclear weapons. Once in a while, he said, he received letters from Americans advocating the use of nuclear weapons to end the war in Korea and, possibly, end the Cold War as well. "For most Americans," he said, "the answer is simple: We are not made that way. We are a moral people. Peace is our goal, with justice and freedom…Starting a war is no way to make peace…Starting an atomic war is totally unthinkable for rational men."

Ideas and ideals would be the weapons of choice in the war with Communism.

"As the free world grows stronger, more united, more attractive to men on both sides of the Iron Curtain—and as Soviet hopes for easy expansion are blocked—then there will have to come a time of change in the Soviet world. Nobody can say for sure when that is going to be, or exactly how it will come about…Whether the Communist rulers shift their policies of their own free will or whether the change comes in some other way, I have not a doubt in the world that a change will occur."

Indeed, he envisioned change—peaceful, progressive change—in the years to come. He told his fellow Americans of his dreams not only for them but for all citizens of the world. "I can't help but dream out loud just a little here," he said as he asked Americans to imagine the "Tigris and Euphrates Valley" blooming "as it did in the times of Babylon." He spoke of turning a plateau in Ethiopia into a new farm belt able to feed a hundred million people. "This is our dream of the future," he said.

As he neared his last moment in the public spotlight, Truman told the nation that he had no regrets, that he had done his best. "When Franklin Roosevelt died, I felt there must be a million men better qualified than I to take up the presidential task," he said. "But the work was mine to do, and I had to do it. And I have tried to give it everything that was in me. Through it all, through all the years I have worked here in this room, I have been well aware I did not really work alone—that you were working with me."

With that, and with his best wishes for his listeners and his country, the man from Independence bade farewell. "And now," he said, "the time has come for me to say good night—and God bless you all."

But he was not quite through. He still had to perform one final role, that of witness to the inauguration of his successor on January 20. If Harry

Truman had even a moment's hesitation about leaving Washington, it was quickly banished. Eisenhower, stewing over Truman's criticism, refused to have lunch with the outgoing president; indeed, he and his wife, Mamie, refused to join the Trumans for a cup of coffee in the White House before they rode together to the Capitol for the inaugural ceremonies. The president-elect remained in his car until the Trumans emerged from the White House to join them for the ride. The trip was short, but it must have seemed so much longer. Conversation between the two presidents was tense and sparse.

Harry and Bess Truman left Washington by train after a farewell lunch hosted by Dean Acheson. They returned to the home of Bess's late mother on Delaware Street in Independence, where they lived out the rest of their years. Old politicians, unlike old soldiers, generally do not fade away, and Harry Truman was no exception. While he embraced private life and sought to live as normal a life as possible, he enthusiastically played the role of elder statesman for his party. He enjoyed visiting universities for lectures, never forgetting that he was too poor to attend college as a young man. Memories of his poor approval ratings faded as the war in Korea ended and the United States became even more prosperous during the 1950s. He returned to the White House for the inauguration of President John Kennedy in 1961, the first time he stepped foot in the mansion since leaving in 1953.

Harry Truman saw history move in his direction, just as he knew it would. In 1965, the influential columnist Joseph Alsop wrote to Truman to admit that many of his criticisms of the Truman years were wrong. Truman replied graciously, saying that he warmly welcomed "your reassessment."[3] Truman and Eisenhower patched up their differences after the assassination of President Kennedy in 1963, an event that left Truman, and the rest of the nation, deeply shaken.

In his final political campaign, he argued, successfully, that former presidents ought to receive an allowance for office expenses. Later, Congress found money to fund pensions for them as well.

He began to fade in the late 1960s and died in 1972 at the age of eighty-eight. He was buried near the presidential library containing his papers and his memories.

Three years later, after the Watergate scandal drove Richard Nixon from the presidency and scarred the office Truman loved, the rock band

Chicago had a hit with a song called "Harry Truman." The country, the song said, was calling for a man who "called a spade a spade like you did back in the days." Jimmy Carter, then running for president on the promise that he would never lie to the American public, told an interviewer that Truman was his favorite president. Actor James Whitmore created a one-man show based on Truman's life.

Yet another Truman revival followed publication of David McCullough's Pulitzer-Prize winning biography in 1992. In the age of political spin and manipulation, Harry Truman's everyman demeanor and plain speaking, so derided in his day, now seemed a welcome antidote to slick promises and empty oratory.

Historians now rank Harry Truman among the nation's greatest presidents. He would be delighted, and he would not be surprised.

Now the party's elder statesman, Harry Truman was Lyndon Johnson's
guest at a ceremony in 1965, when LBJ signed a bill creating the
Medicare system. The aging Truman was seen as a champion
of policies like Medicare, which offered health insurance
to the nation's senior citizens.

Notes

Part One: An Accidental President, 1945–1946

Introduction
[1] David McCullough, *Truman*, 84.

Chapter 1
[1] Harry S. Truman, *Memoirs, Vol. I*, 16.
[2] Ibid., 15.
[3] Ibid., 15.
[4] McCullough, *Truman*, 353.
[5] Ibid., 352.
[6] Harry S. Truman, *Memoirs, Vol. I*, 31.
[7] McCullough, *Truman*, 359.

Chapter 2
[1] Winston Churchill, *Memoirs of the Second World War*, 946.
[2] Ibid., 946.
[3] Marc Trachtenberg, *A Constructed Peace: The Making of the European Settlement*, 11.
[4] McCullough, *Truman*, 351.
[5] Harry S. Truman, *Memoirs, Vol. I*, 126.
[6] Ibid., 373.
[7] Harry S. Truman, *Memoirs, Vol. I*, 93.
[8] Ibid., 99.
[9] Gilbert, *The Day the War Ended*, 95.
[10] Harry S. Truman, *Memoirs, Vol. I*, 231.

Chapter 3
[1] Churchill, *Memoirs of the Second World War*, 967.
[2] McCullough, *Truman*, 382.
[3] Martin Gilbert, *The Day the War Ended: May 8, 1945, Victory in Europe*, 29.
[4] Ibid., 391.
[5] Harry S. Truman, *Memoirs, Vol. I*, 462.
[6] Ibid., 376.
[7] Ibid., 378.
[8] McCullough, *Truman*, 423.
[9] Harry S. Truman, *Memoirs, Vol. I*, 425.
[10] Ibid., 497.

Chapter 4

[1] William E. Pemberton, *Harry S. Truman: Fair Dealer and Cold Warrior*, 64.

[2] Donald R. McCoy, *The Presidency of Harry S. Truman*, 50.

[3] Margaret Truman, *Harry S. Truman*, 318.

Chapter 5

[1] Harry S. Truman, *Memoirs, Vol. I*, 607.

[2] Pemberton, *Harry S. Truman: Fair Dealer and Cold Warrior*, 66.

[3] Harry S. Truman, *Memoirs, Vol. I*, 609.

[4] Pemberton, *Harry S. Truman: Fair Dealer*, 65.

Chapter 6

[1] McCoy, *The Presidency of Harry S. Truman*, 58.

[2] McCullough, *Truman*, 492.

[3] Ibid., 493.

[4] Harry S. Truman, *Memoirs, Vol. I*, 552.

[5] Ibid., 551.

[6] The public papers of Harry S. Truman, May 17, 1946, www.trumanlibrary.org/publicpapers.

[7] McCullough, *Truman*, 497.

[8] Ibid., 500.

[9] Ibid., 506.

Chapter 7

[1] Harry S. Truman, *Memoirs, Vol. II*, 43.

[2] McCoy, *The Presidency of Harry S. Truman*, 65.

[3] The public papers of Harry S. Truman, June 29, 1946, www.trumanlibrary.org/publicpapers.

[4] Ibid.

[5] Robert H. Ferrell, ed., *Off the Record: The Private Papers of Harry S. Truman*, 96.

[6] Ibid., 97.

[7] McCullough, *Truman*, 620.

[8] Harry S. Truman, *Memoirs, Vol. II*, 24–25.

[9] Ferrell, *Off the Record*, 103.

Chapter 8

[1] Ferrell, *Off the Record*, 99.

[2] Harry S. Truman, *Memoirs, Vol. II*, 172.

[3] McCullough, *Truman*, 524.

Part Two: Comeback, 1947–1948

Chapter 9

[1] The public papers of Harry S. Truman, December 31, 1945, www.trumanlibrary.org/publicpapers.

[2] McCullough, *Truman*, 529.
[3] Margaret Truman, *Harry S. Truman*, 351.
[4] Ibid., 351–352.
[5] Ferrell, *Off the Record*, 107.
[6] Ibid., 107.

Chapter 10
[1] Harry S. Truman, *Memoirs, Vol. II*, 100.
[2] Ibid., 102.
[3] Ibid., 103.
[4] Ibid., 104.
[5] McCullough, *Truman*, 545.
[6] Harry S. Truman, *Memoirs, Vol. II*, 105.
[7] Ibid., 105.

Chapter 11
[1] Harry S. Truman, *Memoirs, Vol. II*, 67.
[2] Ibid., 115.
[3] McCullough, *Truman*, 535.
[4] Harry S. Truman, *Memoirs, Vol. II*, 113.
[5] McCullough, *Truman*, 561.
[6] Harry S. Truman, *Memoirs, Vol. II*, 114.
[7] Ibid., 119.
[8] Margaret Truman, *Harry S. Truman*, 320.

Chapter 12
[1] McCullough, *Truman*, 539.
[2] Margaret Truman, *Harry S. Truman*, 383.
[3] Ibid., 383.

Chapter 13
[1] McCullough, *Truman*, 247.
[2] Harry S. Truman, *Memoirs, Vol. II*, 180.
[3] McCullough, *Truman*, 589.

Chapter 14
[1] Irwin Ross, *The Loneliest Campaign*, 26.
[2] McCullough, *Truman*, 584–585.
[3] McCoy, *The Presidency of Harry S. Truman*, 151.
[4] Harry S. Truman, *Memoirs, Vol. II*, 224.
[5] Ibid., 171.
[6] Ibid., 172.

Chapter 15
[1] Ross, *The Loneliest Campaign*, 75.

[2] Harry S. Truman, *Memoirs, Vol. II*, 177.
[3] Ibid., 164–165.
[4] Ross, *The Loneliest Campaign*, 82.
[5] Ibid., 85.
[6] McCullough, *Truman*, 629.
[7] Ross, *The Loneliest Campaign*, 108.
[8] McCullough, *Truman*, 644.

Chapter 16
[1] Ross, *The Loneliest Campaign*, 158.
[2] Harry S. Truman, *Memoirs, Vol. II*, 183.
[3] Ross, *The Loneliest Campaign*, 171.
[4] McCullough, *Truman*, 660.
[5] Ross, *The Loneliest Campaign*, 172.
[6] Ibid., 178.
[7] McCullough, *Truman*, 676.
[8] Ibid., 677.
[9] Ferrell, *Off the Record*, 149–150.
[10] McCullough, *Truman*, 695.
[11] Ibid., 697.
[12] Harry S. Truman, *Memoirs, Vol. II*, 220.

Chapter 17
[1] The public papers of Harry S. Truman, Nov. 1, 1948, www.trumanlibrary.org/publicpapers.
[2] Ross, *The Loneliest Campaign*, 227.
[3] Ibid., 229.

Part Three: A Term of His Own, 1949–1953

Chapter 18

[1] Margaret Truman, *Harry S. Truman*, 436.
[2] Ibid., 436.
[3] The public papers of Harry S. Truman, January 5, 1949, www.trumanlibrary.org/publicpapers.
[4] The public papers of Harry S. Truman, January 20, 1949, www.trumanlibrary.org/publicpapers.

Chapter 19
[1] Harry S. Truman, *Memoirs, Vol. II*, 241.
[2] Ibid., 247.
[3] Trachtenberg, *A Constructed Peace: The Making of the European Settlement*, 87.
[4] McCoy, *The Presidency of Harry S. Truman*, 140.

Chapter 20
[1] Harry S. Truman, *Memoirs, Vol. II*, 131.
[2] The public papers of Harry S. Truman, September 23, 1949, www.trumanlibrary.org/publicpapers.

Chapter 21
[1] McCullough, *Truman*, 768.
[2] McCoy, *The Presidency of Harry S. Truman*, 215.
[3] Harry S. Truman, *Memoirs*, Vol. II, 333.
[4] McCullough, *Truman*, 780.
[5] McCoy, *The Presidency of Harry S. Truman*, 224.
[6] Ibid., 226.

Chapter 22
[1] McCullough, *Truman*, 805.
[2] Harry S. Truman, *Memoirs, Vol. II*, 384.
[3] Margaret Truman, *Harry S. Truman*, 547–548.
[4] Ibid., 547.
[5] Ibid., 547.
[6] Harry S. Truman, *Memoirs, Vol. II*, 442.
[7] McCullough, *Truman*, 838.
[8] Ferrell, *Off the Record*, 210–211.
[9] Harry S. Truman, *Memoirs, Vol. II*, 449.

Chapter 23
[1] Ferrell, *Off the Record*, 211.
[2] Ibid., 211.
[3] Ibid., 232.
[4] The public papers of Harry S. Truman, March 29, 1952, www.trumanlibrary.org/publicpapers.
[5] Harry S. Truman, *Memoirs, Vol. II*, 468.
[6] McCullough, *Truman*, 902.

Chapter 24
[1] McCullough, *Truman*, 911.
[2] Ferrell, *Off the Record*, 272.
[3] Ibid., 268–269.
[4] Ibid., 275–276.
[5] Ibid., 279.

Chapter 25
[1] Ferrell, *Off the Record*, 287.
[2] Margaret Truman, *Harry S. Truman*, 608.
[3] Ferrell, *Off the Record*, 410.

Bibliography

Churchill, Winston S. *Memoirs of the Second World War*. New York: Bonanza Books, 1978.

Ferrell, Robert H., ed. *Off the Record: The Private Papers of Harry S. Truman*. New York: Harper and Row, 1980.

Flynn, Edward J. *You're the Boss: The Practice of American Politics*. New York: Collier Books, 1962.

Gilbert, Martin. *The Day the War Ended: May 8, 1945, Victory in Europe*. New York: Henry Holt, 1995.

McCoy, Donald R. *The Presidency of Harry S. Truman*. Lawrence, KS: University Press of Kansas, 1989.

McCullough, David. *Truman*. New York: Simon & Schuster, 1992.

Pemberton, William E. *Harry S. Truman: Fair Dealer and Cold Warrior*. Boston: Twayne Publishers, 1989.

Ross, Irwin. *The Loneliest Campaign: The Truman Victory of 1948*. New York: Signet, 1968.

Trachtenberg, Marc. *A Constructed Peace: The Making of the European Settlement, 1945–1963*. Princeton, NJ: Princeton University Press, 1999.

Truman, Harry S. *Memoirs, Vol. I, 1945, Year of Decisions*. New York: Signet, 1955.

———. *Memoirs, Vol. II, Years of Trial and Hope*. Garden City, NY: Doubleday & Company, 1956.

Truman, Margaret. *Harry S. Truman*. New York: Pocket Books, 1974.

Index

B

C

Credits

Photos have been obtained with the kind assistance of the Harry S. Truman Library and Museum (located in Independence, MO), the National Archives, and the Library of Congress. All photos are in the public domain.

The full version of most of the speeches selected can be accessed at www.trumanlibrary.org/audio/audio.htm.

Audio segments have been edited for time and content. In the interest of clarity and accuracy, all edits within each speech are made apparent by the fading out of the audio, then the fading in of the next segment. While we have attempted to achieve the best possible quality on this archival material, some audio quality is the result of source limitations.

For a wealth of information about Harry Truman, visit the website of the Harry S. Truman Library and Museum at http://www.trumanlibrary.org.

About Sourcebooks MediaFusion

Launched with the 1998 *New York Times* bestseller *We Interrupt This Broadcast* and formally founded in 2000, Sourcebooks MediaFusion is the nation's leading publisher of mixed-media books. This revolutionary imprint is dedicated to creating original content—be it audio, video, CD-Rom, or Web-based—that is fully integrated with the books we create. The result, we hope, is a new, richer, eye-opening experience with books for our readers. Our experiential books have become both bestsellers and classics in their subjects, including poetry (*The 100 Best African American Poems*), children's books (*The Tree That Time Built*), history (*My Fellow Americans*), sports (*The Greatest Moments in Sports*), the plays of William Shakespeare, and more. See what's new from us at www.sourcebooks.com.

Acknowledgments

This is my fourth book with Sourcebooks. My thanks to Todd Stocke, Stephen O'Rear, Anne Hartman, and April Sirianni for their insights and assistance.

The staff at the Harry S. Truman Library and Museum in Independence, MO, particularly Janice Davis, was essential to the completion of this project.

As always, my thanks to John Wright, Eileen Duggan, and Kate and Connor Golway.

About the Author

Terry Golway is curator of the John Kean Center for American History at Kean University in Union, New Jersey. This is his fourth book on presidential speeches, along with *Together We Cannot Fail* (FDR), *Ronald Reagan's America*, and *Let Every Nation Know* (JFK). He is also the author of *Washington's General*, a biography of Nathanael Greene, and writes for the *New York Times*, *American Heritage*, and the *New York Observer*. He lives in Maplewood, New Jersey.